Inside
Drucker's
Brain

Inside Drucker's Brain

Jeffrey A. Krames

Portfolio

PORTFOLIO

Published by the Penguin Group

Penguin Group (USA) Inc., 375 Hudson Street, New York, New York 10014, U.S.A. ● Penguin Group (Canada), 90 Eglinton Avenue East, Suite 700, Toronto, Ontario, Canada M4P 2Y3 (a division of Pearson Penguin Canada Inc.) ● Penguin Books Ltd, 80 Strand, London WC2R 0RL, England ● Penguin Ireland, 25 St. Stephen's Green, Dublin 2, Ireland (a division of Penguin Books Ltd) ● Penguin Books Australia Ltd, 250 Camberwell Road, Camberwell, Victoria 3124, Australia ● (a division of Pearson Australia Group Pty Ltd) Penguin Books India Pvt Ltd, 11 Community Centre, Panchsheel Park, New Delhi – 110 017, India ● Penguin Group (NZ), 67 Apollo Drive, Rosedale, North Shore 0632, New Zealand (a division of Pearson New Zealand Ltd) ● Penguin Books (South Africa) (Pty) Ltd, 24 Sturdee Avenue, Rosebank, Johannesburg 2196, South Africa

Penguin Books Ltd, Registered Offices:
80 Strand, London WC2R 0RL, England

First published in 2008 by Portfolio,
a member of Penguin Group (USA) Inc.

10   9   8   7   6   5   4   3   2   1

LIBRARY OF CONGRESS CATALOGING IN PUBLICATION DATA
Krames, Jeffrey A.
Inside Drucker's brain / Jeffrey A. Krames.
     p.   cm.
Includes bibliographical references and index.
 ISBN 978-1-59184-222-4
1. Drucker, Peter F. (Peter Ferdinand), 1909–2005   2. Industrial management.
I. Title
HD31.D776K73 2008
658.0092—dc22   2008022621

Printed in the United States of America
Set in Vendetta with Myriad Pro
Designed by Daniel Lagin

To Peter F. Drucker, for opening his home to me,
and sharing his wisdom.

Contents

Inside
Drucker's
Brain

Introduction

In Search of Drucker

Early November 2003: The last person I expected to hear from that Monday morning was Peter Drucker. After all, I never contacted him directly and to this day have no idea how he got my number. As a book editor and publisher of twenty-plus years I routinely spoke with many prominent authors, but this was *Drucker.*

I tried to grasp what he was saying. He was only a month shy of his ninety-fourth birthday and both his speech—difficult to understand with his thick Viennese accent—and his hearing were not what they once were. He spoke too loudly and even though I practically shouted my responses into the phone he could not hear me. He was obviously upset and it didn't take much to figure out that I was the one who had upset him.

A bit of history: after editing and writing several books on Jack Welch (the former CEO of GE), I had been seriously pondering a Drucker book for four years. Many of Welch's best ideas had originated with Drucker—as had those of a host of other business practitioners and authors—and I thought it was time to go straight to the source.

Although Drucker had written three dozen books on business and society, I thought the definitive book on Drucker had not yet been written. I had no intention of writing a biography, but rather a book that would accomplish two important objectives: one, to showcase his most important management philosophies and signature strategies, and show how they are as useful today as they were when Drucker first espoused them; and two, to reveal how many of the best-selling business books of the last two decades were built on ideas that he originated. I regard Drucker's primary contribution to be as much a mindset as it is a methodology. Drucker is all about getting managers to ask the right questions. To see beyond what they think they know, to look past yesterday so that they might get a glimpse of tomorrow.

Although he caught me off guard that morning, Drucker had not called me completely out of the blue. I had initiated contact first—not with him, but with one of his publishers. That was partly because Drucker had a reputation as being one who policed his works and copyrights as vigorously as any aggressive attorney, and I thought securing permission to use *any* of his previously published works was going to be an uphill battle. To test the waters, I selected excerpts from a single book and sent off a permission request to the publishing house.

I was surprised when Truman Talley, the publisher of the

book in question, sent me a permission to use the material for a fee of two hundred dollars. *That was easy,* I thought to myself. However, I did not know what I had unwittingly set in motion. After granting the permission, the publisher must have contacted Drucker, who held the copyright to all his works, to let him know what they had done.

A few days after I received the permission letter strange things started to happen. My wife said that she had begun receiving crank calls at the house while I was at work.

"What kind of calls?" I asked. She really could not describe them other than to say that she could not understand a word of whatever the caller was saying.

"So I hung up on him," she explained, shrugging the incidents off. This happened several times before I got the call the next week from the same man I immediately recognized as anything but a crank caller. And it didn't take long to realize that my wife had done the unthinkable: she had hung up on Peter Drucker, and more than once!

Since Drucker could not hear me on the phone that morning, I asked if I could send him a letter to clear up things. In the first of what would be several letters to Drucker, I explained in depth the book I intended to write. I also told him that I would designate him as the inventor of management, a moniker he had denied for decades (but now made no effort to disavow).

Drucker and I corresponded for two months. We exchanged a few letters about the book and the approach I intended to take. In mid-November, Drucker sent me a letter that granted me permission to quote from any and all of his books, and shortly thereafter invited me to interview him at his home in Claremont, California.

We set the dates of the interview for December 22 and December 23, a two-day period that would include a far-ranging discussion of topics. I asked Drucker if he would like to see the questions I intended to ask in advance. He said yes, so I spent much of a week polishing a list of some two dozen questions that I thought most pertinent to the theme of the book. When I asked Drucker if the questions were satisfactory, he said, "Yes and no."

"The questions are fine," he wrote. "But there are far too many of them." Drucker then asked me to reduce the number to a maximum of six. I was taken aback. How could we spend two days with only five or six questions to discuss? Clearly, I did not yet "get" Drucker, who I would later learn could fashion a day's discourse around any subject, from management to society to Japanese art.

D-day: Monday, December 22, 2003, 5:40 a.m. I awoke to the sounds of large aircraft speeding down runways and for a few seconds forgot where I was. It took a few moments to collect myself. It was the kind of cloudless, blue-sky December morning one finds only in Southern California, thousands of miles from the sleet in Chicago.

As I quickly showered and then dressed in suit and tie, I realized, not without irony, that I knew little about Peter Drucker the man. I knew a great deal about his writings, his business philosophy, his management tenets, having read—more than once—the vast majority of his thirty-five books on management, and management and society. (Drucker wrote extensively about the relationship between management and society.) Even his beefy memoir, *Adventures of a Bystander*, revealed little about who he *really* was (see the Epilogue for some highlights from that book).

I grabbed the two tape recorders I had brought with me, the car keys, and the books, and headed out to the rental car. I could not help but reflect wryly on how I had gotten here. To people in the business book industry, Drucker was a singular figure: the man who had more or less discovered the discipline of management and become its chronicler. But Drucker had many critics who felt he had lost his edge—and relevance. And it wasn't only the usual suspects, such as the academic elite, who regarded Drucker as a has-been or an almost-was. The dean of the Peter F. Drucker Graduate School of Management at Claremont Graduate University* later told *BusinessWeek*'s John Byrne, "This [Drucker] is a brand in decline."

Drucker, who was incredibly self-aware and no less so now, surely had heard similar rumblings. I suspected that he had his legacy in mind when he agreed to my request for an interview.

I knew the criticism of Drucker was unfounded. After many

---

* In 2003 the school was renamed the Peter F. Drucker and Masatoshi Ito Graduate School of Management.

hundreds of hours of research, it became increasingly clear that the popular press and the academic elite had gotten it wrong. His writings served as the foundation for a great number of business best sellers published during the post-1980 business book boom.

Tom Peters, author of *In Search of Excellence*, one of the two management books that launched the modern day boom, said, "No true discipline of management existed before Drucker." He also said: "He [Drucker] was the creator and inventor of modern management. In the early 1950s, nobody had a tool kit to manage these incredibly complex organizations that had gone out of control. Drucker was the first person to give us a handbook for that." Incredibly, Peters also reportedly said, "everything we have written" in *In Search of Excellence* could be found "in some corner or other" of *The Practice of Management*.

A noteworthy management and organizational behavior expert, Charles Handy, said, "Virtually everything can be traced back to Drucker," and Jim Collins (*Good to Great*), another exceptional business author, acknowledged Drucker's contributions as well, calling him "the leading founder of the field of management." He also wrote that Drucker's "primary contribution is not a single idea, but rather an entire body of work that has one gigantic advantage: nearly all of it is essentially right."

There were other noteworthy authors who acknowledged Drucker's contributions, including Michael Hammer, author of the mega best seller *Reengineering the Corporation*, who considered Drucker a hero. Hammer told another consultant and author,* "It is with some trepidation that I open his early books, because I am afraid that I will discover that he has anticipated my latest ideas by a matter of several decades. It is all there."

Other business best sellers contain seeds that were planted by Drucker years earlier. In addition to Michael Hammer and James Champy's *Reengineering the Corporation*, these include Marcus Buckingham and Donald Clifton's *Now Discover Your Strengths*, Clayton Christensen's *The Innovator's Dilemma* and *The Innovator's Solution*, Richard Nolan and David Croson's *Creative Destruction*, and Larry Bossidy and Ram Charan's *Execution*, to name a few. Drucker's influence on the ideas that shaped these books and others will be examined in depth throughout this one. "It is frustratingly difficult to cite a significant modern management concept that was not first articulated, if not invented, by Drucker," asserted James O'Toole, the noted management expert who recently served as managing director of the Booz Allen Hamilton Strategic Leadership Center and chair of the center's academic Board of Advisers. "I say that with both awe and dismay."

Business leaders such as Michael Dell, Intel founder Andy Grove, and Microsoft founder Bill Gates also praised Drucker (when asked who he read, Gates replied, *"Well, Drucker, of*

---

* The consultant-author was Elizabeth Haas Edersheim, author of *The Definitive Drucker* (McGraw-Hill, 2007).

course."). Most business authors, however, often unaware of his deep-rooted influence on their work, were less inclined to credit him. Drucker told me it didn't bother him at all. He inspired scores of business book authors, and I believe that's what he wanted his legacy to be: he wanted his ideas to be used in forms that could be implemented over the generations. He wanted to make a difference.

While it is clear that Drucker had it right from the start, the vast majority of people were still not listening to him. His breakthrough book was aptly titled *The Practice of Management* because it was the first book ever published that showed managers how to manage. *"Before that, there was nothing… nothing had come together,"* Drucker said. Yet, if one believes much of what was written of him after say, 1990, one gets the distinct impression that Drucker's influence was little more than a fad. For example, today's management textbooks contain little more than a Drucker footnote or two. In places that matter most, his contributions to the management field are very hard to find.

Drucker, who never lost his humility, was never one to blow his own horn. When asked his profession, he answered simply: "I am a writer." When this "writer" had a new idea, he simply wrote a new book. He told me that he never read his previous works. His publisher may have repackaged some of his earlier books, but his entire career—not to mention his entire perspective—was based on looking forward, not back. Abandoning yesterday wasn't merely one of his management principles, it had become part of Drucker's DNA.

En route to Drucker's home, I thought about how Drucker seldom cooperated with authors, having once said, "One of the secrets of keeping young is not to give interviews but to stick to one's work—and that's what I'm doing. Sorry, I am not available." Drucker clamped down on any author or publisher who had the audacity to borrow material from his books without his express written permission. During our brief period of correspondence, Drucker wrote me that he only played the role of vigilant watchdog after a Harvard Business School professor used three chapters of one of his books without permission or attribution.

Drucker also had a drawerful of postcards, addressed from his "secretary" (*he* was his secretary), which could be sent to anyone requesting an endorsement or interview: "Mr. Peter F. Drucker appreciates your kind interest, but he is unable to contribute articles or forewords . . . give interviews, comment on manuscript. . . ." Three years earlier I was on the receiving end of one of those missives when I had asked him to endorse my first book.

I was due at his home at ten that Monday morning, and allowed an extra forty minutes in case the MapQuest directions faxed to me by Drucker led me astray. But I had led myself astray. I had been so deep in thought that I missed the turnoff to his home by several miles. I nervously retraced my route, found the right street, and pulled up to the right address at four minutes to ten.

I stared at the house for several moments. The unimpressive home was far too unassuming, the type of house one could find in any quiet American suburb. It was a nice enough home, surrounded by neatly kept gardens, but it seemed past its prime, a bit faded. Could this really be where he lived?

But of course this was Drucker's home. The management thinker had no time, and less inclination, to ever trade up to a more lavish home. It reminded me of the story of Albert Einstein's suits. I once read that they were all identical, ensuring he would never waste a moment on such a frivolous decision as to what to wear.

I collected the tape recorders, the books, and my briefcase, and knocked on the door just before ten. I had confirmed this appointment several times, and Drucker assured me that he had set the time aside for the two-day interview. I had come two thousand miles to meet him, so the thought that he would not be there never entered my mind. That was about to change.

When knocking yielded no results, I rang the bell. A minute or two passed, then three, four, and five. Nothing. Surely I had gotten the day right. After several minutes (which felt more like an hour), I returned to my car to search for my cell phone. I could not believe it. I had been looking forward to this day for months, arranged and confirmed every detail, but so far Drucker was nowhere to be found.

After a dozen or so rings, Drucker finally answered the phone and said he would "be down" in a few minutes. When he greeted me at the door he explained that his hearing aid was either not in or turned off.

Drucker had celebrated his ninety-fourth birthday the month before, and he looked every one of those years. He appeared thin and frail. His glasses were thicker than I had imagined, and his hearing aids more conspicuous. However, it did not take long to discern the sharp mind behind the bespectacled, aged face. He moved with a cane, and far more slowly than I had anticipated. He was wearing a multicolored sweater and a sports jacket, but he looked cold, despite the warmth of the day. He seemed to have little strength when he greeted me with something less than a firm handshake. Even though we had exchanged several warm letters during the past few weeks, I felt like an intruder. That feeling changed as the day went on.

He showed me to his sitting room, and led me to a table that offered a view of a swimming pool that appeared as if it had not been used in years. With the drapes mostly drawn, the room was half eclipsed in darkness, so Drucker pointed to two lamps that would help the situation. After switching them on, I took the chair he indicated and he sat close by, only a few feet away. He later told me that I was sitting in the same chair Jack Welch had sat in weeks before he became CEO of GE in 1981.

I placed the two tape recorders and the small stack of books on the table that stood between us. I had brought half a dozen of Drucker's books, in case I wanted to reference them. Drucker would later sign each of them without my prompting.

There was little small talk; we launched right into it. Correction: *he* launched right into it. Although I immediately took out the page with the six questions we had agreed to and placed it on the table between us, we did not refer to them even once the entire day.

He had his own agenda, and was anxious to get started. When he began to talk I reached for the tape recorders, but he asked me not to turn them on. I reached for the tape recorders several times before he grudgingly gave in and signaled me to switch them on. To this day I have no idea why Drucker shunned the tape recorders. Perhaps it had something to do with his accent. He sounded more like a German physicist than the management thinker who had ignited a discipline. He also coughed frequently, which slowed things down.

I thought I would be nervous, but I wasn't; I was simply too immersed in making sure I did not waste a minute of my time with him. Drucker's poor hearing demanded that I repeat most of my questions and responses twice. "What?" was the most common Drucker answer to any question. That left very little room for humor, as I was focused on making sure he understood me. However, his self-deprecating humor was one constant throughout the day. His humility was authentic and impressive.

He started by telling me the story of his early days in Europe and how he later got into the management field "totally by accident," by "falling into it." He explained how he never managed anything. "I am the world's worst manager," he declared sardonically with a slight smile. That last fact, that he never managed anything, either amused him or irked him. It was difficult to tell which.

He also told the story of how his first business book isolated him from any traditional career path right from the start. The book, *Concept of the Corporation*, was published in 1946 and contained the first large-scale study of a major U.S. corporation: General Motors. The book was an immediate best seller in the United States and Japan, and made him something of an instant icon. However, publishing a popular book, which by definition back then meant a frivolous book, was no way to advance a career. Drucker's friend, the president of Bennington College, told him: "Peter, this book is neither government nor economics, where will you be going?" "He was absolutely right," said Drucker.

Of course, Peter Drucker would make his own way. Neither Harvard nor Stanford would ever appear on his résumé, but he had no regrets: "I had turned down the Harvard Business School," he explained to me. "It was very clear that I didn't belong there. And also I wanted to do my own writing and my own consulting; you were not allowed to do consulting in those days at the Business School. And you were supposed to write cases, for which I never had the slightest use, personally."

That morning with Drucker was one I'll never forget. We worked without a break until noon. He suggested lunch at his favorite Italian bistro in town, so we left his home and I assisted him into the rental car, glad that I had sprung for the full-sized up-grade. He gave me a quick tour of the town, which included the Peter F. Drucker Graduate School of Management at Claremont University.

We had to park about a block from the restaurant, as it was full of students and parking was tight. Drucker took my arm whenever he had to walk more than a few yards. On that day I learned to hate what age did to people.

We worked through lunch, at least part of it. I had the tape recorder going and we continued our interview as he ate his pasta. He also told me about his large family, his very bright children, whom I figured all to be well past middle age, and how they took little or no interest in what their father did for a living. I could not believe it. Their father was the inventor of manage-ment and they were too busy with their own professional lives to take note of it. But to Drucker, who never lost his European bearing, it seemed only natural that his children would be doc-tors and professionals and go their own way. He said he would have been surprised if they had shown anything but a passing interest in his work.

During lunch he exhibited the only lapse of memory I ob-served during my entire time with him. He ordered his entrée confidently enough, but when the waitress brought it, he in-sisted that he had ordered something else. It took him only a few moments to realize his error. Other than that, his mind was as clear as ever, as was confirmed by his quick-witted responses to all of my queries and his razor-sharp memories of years past.

After lunch Peter asked if I would mind helping him to run an errand. "Not at all," I said. "Just say where." He came back quickly: "I need to buy a Christmas present for my wife." He had been married to his wife, Doris, for seventy years. I knew her to be a successful author and entrepreneur who had studied at the London School of Economics. As I waited in the car outside the local confectioner's shop for Peter to buy her chocolates ("I always buy her chocolates," he had confessed), I suddenly realized that I had not seen Doris even once that morning.

After the long wait (it was three days before Christmas and the entire town seemed to want chocolates), we returned to his home and picked up where we had left off. Having discussed much of his biography in the morning, we were able to delve into some other compelling topics (also not on the agenda). As a business book editor and publisher, it wasn't often I had the chance to sit with one of the best-selling authors of my industry. So it was only natural that I would ask him about publishing.

He confessed that he had been more wrong about publishing than anything else in his life. There was that self-deprecating humor again. He might have been wrong in many of his predictions about publishing, but he certainly knew all about the *history* of publishing. In fact, he knew more about a whole range of topics than most anyone I've met.

In our afternoon session he showed me a prime example when he spoke about publishing. He first explained that his own name, Drucker, when translated into English, meant "printer." He then spoke of his ancestors: "My family were printers in Amsterdam ... they were printers to one of the biggest churches ... their biggest moneymaker was the Koran; they printed Korans for the Dutch East India Company." (Founded in 1602, the Dutch East India Company was the world's first multinational corporation.)

The fact that publishing was not included in our agreed upon list of questions says a good deal about our day together, and something important about Drucker as well. He had no use for scripts, preferring to talk off the cuff and about the topics that interested him most. He never considered himself to be an interesting subject ("I'm totally uninteresting," he told an interviewer*), but on the day of our interview he broke with tradition when he discussed his life at length.

After a few moments, it was no longer Peter Drucker but Professor Drucker who took over. He loved to talk about the history of the written word. The first printed novel—*Don Quixote*—appeared in 1600 or 1605, he said, and that was made possible by movable type. He then explained to me that the great innovations in color printing had taken place in Antwerp, no Paris, he said, quickly correcting himself, at the end of the sixteenth century. Someone had merged the new technology of lithograph with the new technology of printing and that had produced the first illustrated book. But he quickly added, the contents did not change for two hundred years. The appearance

---

* That interviewer was John Byrne.

and design changed, but the contents of the book did not change until the end of the seventeenth century.

Then he fast-forwarded a few hundred years to describe a book he was publishing in the upcoming year, "a book in which most of the page will be empty, so that the reader is a user not just a reader, but a user," he said. Drucker published two additional books before his death in 2005, one that had more white space than words on each page (*The Daily Drucker*) and the other a workbooklike version of one of his classics (*The Effective Executive in Action*). Publishing books like this would have been unthinkable only a few years earlier. But the world of publishing had changed and Drucker had changed with it.

He went on to describe online publishing at length, and how that was changing the landscape of the industry. A friend of his was writing a medical book, which he described: "It is formatted so that it can be displayed on the computer so it could be made interactive . . . while it is not meant to be displayed at the computer, it is formatted as if it already were. The publisher has come back and said we want another blank page. . . . They said they want to have space for the user."

As our interview wound down a few minutes after four that afternoon, the only interruption of the day stormed into the room. It was Doris, his wife, who immediately asked me to leave because she was afraid that her husband had exerted himself too much. Evidently she had heard him coughing more frequently toward the end of the day. (I had asked him how he was every few minutes and he had insisted that he was fine.) I felt awful and hoped that I had done nothing that could bring him ill health.

I had only time enough to gather up my things, and as I did, I heard Doris and Peter Drucker talking. I suddenly got a bad feeling. It didn't take long for me to realize that it was about to be *my* turn to abandon something. Doris insisted that after the very full day Peter and I had spent together, he needed the next day for rest, so the second half-day session we had planned was out of the question. I had brought along a camera for a snapshot of me with Drucker, but Doris wouldn't hear of it. I had only a few moments to thank Drucker for all he had done, gather up my things, and head for the door.

It was upsetting, to say the least. As I drove back to the airport Sheraton, I quickly reviewed the interview in my mind. I was afraid that I hadn't gotten it, hadn't gotten the answers to the questions I thought were most important. As it would turn out, my fears were unfounded. I had actually gotten far more than I had bargained for. Despite his years, Drucker was in rare form that day, and he had given one incredible interview. Although I did not know it at the time, that interview would affect me deeply over the next several years.

It took many months for me to transcribe the six-hour-plus taped interview, but the lessons I learned were not immediately clear. I had to allow some months, even years, for them to sink in. I learned more about Drucker that day—and the real essence of management—than I had during the many years I had read him and other seminal figures in the field. In twenty-plus years I had published management books by countless authors. Yet not one gave me the education I had gained at Drucker's side in that one remarkable day.

His lessons delved into the areas of education, society, politics, and medicine. Drucker was the ultimate Renaissance man, and when he died, an enormous body of knowledge died with him.

Drucker lived a life based on embracing tomorrow and abandoning yesterday. Along the way he discovered an important paradox: in order to build, one must tear down. Drucker had little difficulty tearing things down, abandoning what did not work, leaving behind what was no longer important. That was how he was able to accomplish so much.

The chief goal of *Inside Drucker's Brain* is to give readers a fresh perspective into the thought patterns of this extraordinary thinker. At the same time, by including many contemporary examples, I hope to bring a part of Drucker's incredible body of knowledge to life, and show how so many of his seminal ideas are as relevant today as when they were written.

The following chapters contain the essence of what Drucker passed on to me that day. They also showcase many seminal management and leadership insights and strategies. Peter Drucker amassed an unprecedented archive comprised of many hundreds of thousands of pages. The pages that follow will give readers a key to Drucker's world, one in which tomorrow always comes first.

Chapter 1

Opportunity Favors the Prepared Mind

"Peter, you have ruined your academic career forever."

—What Drucker's friend told him after he published
Concept of the Corporation

As I sat with Drucker that morning, it occurred to me that the inside of his home was similar to the outside: understated and uncluttered, with books and Japanese art and neutral-colored couches and chairs. There was no evidence of a trophy room, or even a trophy corner.

Drucker's writing career had started almost sixty-five years earlier, with the publication of *The End of Economic Man* (1939), an antifascism book that attracted the attention and praise of Winston Churchill. Since then he had been hailed by U.S. presidents (for example, Nixon), and had won the Presidential Medal of Freedom in 2002 (awarded by George W. Bush), yet there was nothing in sight that indicated anything of these accomplishments. As I took in the surroundings I reminded myself to focus on the job at hand. It was not enough that the tape recorders were working; I needed to pay close attention if I was to engage Drucker by asking the right follow-up questions.

However, Drucker never allowed me to get in that first question. He was like the football coach who had arrived on the sidelines with the first twenty plays already decided upon, and didn't waste a moment getting to it. His first order of business was to describe his serendipitous entry into the business world. Drucker explained at length how he accidentally got into the management field (*but he* created *the management field,* I thought to myself). At first it seemed as though Drucker was having a bit of fun with me—a career like Drucker's does not happen by accident. But as he narrated story after story, I realized that there was no false or calculated humility. He meant it when he said he "fell into management."

Drucker told me he didn't know anything about management from "the inside" because he had never been a manager. It wasn't that he wasn't interested in business. Before coming to the United States he held several jobs that had immersed him in different parts of the business world: "I was a trainee in what had become the European headquarters of a major Wall Street firm that's long gone . . . one of those great nineteenth-century German/Jewish American firms. I was a trainee in the first investment department in Europe . . . that was an American Invention," said Drucker.

However, Drucker's timing could not have been worse. The stock market crashed at about the same time he started, putting an end to any hopes of an investment banking career: "I was last in and first out when the market crashed," reported Drucker good-naturedly.

As luck would have it, just after he was fired, a colleague invited Drucker for a drive to a local newspaper. There the publisher told the jobless young man that they were looking for a business and foreign affairs editor. "And an hour later I was hired without any business experience," recounted Drucker. "I was a trainee in Hamburg for eighteen months where I mostly learned to spell Edinburgh, literally. All I did for eighteen months was to write out envelopes!"

Drucker handled more than envelopes when he left Hamburg to work as a reporter a few years later: "I had gotten to know quite a few companies when I was the American business writer for a group of British newspapers in Frankfurt"—one of those newspapers was the precursor to *The Financial Times*. He also received his doctorate in public and international law while holding down his reporting job.

He then worked as an economist for an international bank in London. But that was it, said Drucker, "That's my total business experience ... I spent two, almost three years in London as the economist asset manager over a small and fast-growing investment bank ... but I have no other business experience."

After a few moments of silence (it was so quiet I could hear the whirring of the tape recorder), I reminded Drucker that he had more business experience than that. "You are a management consultant," I added, to which Drucker quickly replied: "A consultant has no risk…the only risk he has is that the client doesn't come back. *The clients pay for the consultant's mistakes,*" he said finally, as if to put an end to that discussion once and for all.

Drucker's Break

Drucker came to the United States in 1937, and began his career as professor of politics and philosophy at a liberal arts college in Vermont, Bennington College. However, if he had had his way he would not have taught either of those courses. He confided to me that he would have preferred to teach the freshman writing course. He said he had known he could write since he was twelve, and in English, since "we grew up multilingual. At home we spoke German and English, more English than German."

It was while teaching at Bennington College that he got the break that would forever alter his life's course. It started with a phone call he received in the fall of 1943. Almost exactly to the day, sixty years later, Peter Drucker retold the story in vivid detail, recounting each detail as if it had taken place six weeks earlier rather than six decades.

The Phone Call That Sparked a Discipline

"To this day I don't know how General Motors came to me or who was responsible for it," started Drucker, looking off in another direction. "We had been up in Vermont since the summer of 1941 and the college closed down in the winter. We had rented an apartment near Columbia and I tried to find out in the library how corporations are … managed … *but I could find nothing on the topic.*

"And nobody was willing to let me come in [to study the internal workings of a large corporation] until finally … probably exactly to the day, sixty years ago, a telephone call came in and the voice said, 'I am Paul Garrett; I am a vice president of General Motors in charge of public relations and I have been asked to ask you whether you'd be willing to make a study of our top management.' I have never been able to find out who it was at GM who wanted me to do this—everybody denied it.

"I asked [before I committed myself] if I could make a tour of the company … I then came back to the then vice chairman, who probably was the man who had the idea to bring me in, Donaldson Brown. And I said, Mr. Brown, I can't do this study. Nobody will want to talk to me; they will see me as a top management spy … and I said to him there is only one way [that this will work]. In this united country you can do anything if you say you are writing a book. He said no, we are not going to have it.

"And so we parted … after six weeks Paul Garrett called back and said we have been thinking about it; come back to Detroit to discuss it, and so we agreed on me writing a book … I told GM I will not have it censored by you except for actual facts … that's how I began and I spent the next eighteen months or so … I think I visited every GM Division east of the Rockies. I wrote the report and GM said you have to publish it; we committed ourselves to it. I had a publisher but nobody thought that such a book would have any market.

"My publisher only published it because he had published two earlier books of mine that had been successful ... It was a tremendous success. That's how I got into management ... *But I really don't know anything about it from the inside.*"

It was the publication of that book, *Concept of the Corporation* (1946), that gave people the first up close look at the inner workings of General Motors, or any large corporation, warts and all. That watershed book, which argued for decentralization—the process of delegating decision making down into an organization, closer to the people who actually do the work—would gain greater traction in the decades ahead.

Decentralization was one of the major themes of that book and other Drucker works. He felt strongly that a large company with a few key executives barking out orders for the entire company, no matter how widely dispersed its operations, was a recipe for failure.

By the 1980s, Drucker had inspired more than three quarters of Fortune 500 companies to become decentralized. He had also made a cogent argument for the humanization of the worker. Up to that point, employees were dehumanized, treated as cogs or "helpers," considered a cost, not an asset.

Drucker also argued that workers should be empowered to make more decisions, arguing for "creating the self-governing plant community." He described in detail the relationship between the individual and the organization, which became the nucleus of so many future business books; yet few of today's business authors have read that more than sixty-year-old work, which I call the grandfather of the modern-day business book.

Publication of *Concept of the Corporation* put Drucker on a path he would not veer from for the rest of his life. But it was not a traditional path; in fact, as this story illustrates, Drucker found himself deep in uncharted waters following the book's publication.

"*Concept of the Corporation* established business as a subject of study," Drucker told me. But as his friend the president of Bennington College told him, it nearly ruined him. To get ahead in the academic world, one did research, published papers, and got tenure. One harsh reviewer at the time wished this "promising young scholar will now devote his considerable talents to a more respectable subject."

The more prestigious the institution, the greater the likelihood the faculty would thumb their noses at Drucker's commerical books. All books were considered to be frivolous, a distraction from the things that serious academics were supposed to do to advance their careers (that still holds true today in top-tier and most four-year universities). Drucker understood this and plowed on, damn the consequences.

It is not without irony that his success as an author worked against him. But Drucker was never concerned with conforming to convention. To the contrary, from his earliest days he showed a propensity for abandoning the old and charting a new path. He never cared what people thought. He also exhibited great courage.

In his early twenties, shortly after Hitler came to power,

Drucker wrote two small books, pamphlets really, that he knew would be banned and burned by the Nazis. He told me, "I happen not to be Jewish, though of Jewish descent. But quite a few generations back." But Drucker did not write these books because of his Jewish ancestry; he did it because it was important to him to be counted, so that at least he would know he had taken a stand against tyranny, hatred, and fascism (see the Epilogue for more details on this period of his life).

Fired by Eisenhower

By 1950, Drucker had left Bennington and was supposed to take a teaching position at Columbia University. However, that was not meant to be. Once again fate intervened. Here is how he recalled his "accidental" teaching career: "I had begun to teach, again by pure accident, at the Graduate Business School of New York University in 1950 . . . ; a year before that I had turned down the Harvard Business School."

Drucker was not willing to give up his burgeoning consulting business, which would have been necessary if he had chosen to teach at Harvard. And he hated writing cases, and the Harvard Business School was known for its case approach.

So Harvard was out. Instead, Drucker signed on to teach at Columbia, in New York, but Dwight D. Eisenhower, who was president of the college then—and not yet president of the country— "was a cost cutter," so Drucker's job was eliminated before he'd set foot inside a lecture hall.

Minutes after getting the bad news about the Columbia job, he ran into someone he knew on the way to a subway station in New York. That chance meeting, like many other random events in Drucker's life, proved auspicious. Here's how Drucker remembered that accidental meeting: "My friend said, 'What are you doing?' And I said, 'I just found out that I don't have a job at Columbia.' And I said to him, 'What are you doing?' And he said, 'I am coming to raid the Columbia Business School for people to teach at our graduate business school …,' and before we reached the subway station I had signed on at NYU."

Of course, no one attains Drucker's level of success by accident. When I asked him if he really achieved so much by sheer luck or happenstance, his voice and manner instantly took on a more serious tone: *"Opportunity favors the prepared mind. If opportunity knocks at the door you have to open it. You have to be receptive to it and I was."*

Opportunity Favors the Prepared Mind

Each step of Drucker's career put him in uncharted waters. He never turned his back on a favorable opportunity if he felt it was the right one. Rather, he maintained the flexibility to take advantage of opportunities as they came his way. He did it by abandoning the tried and true in favor of an uncertain future. Put another way, sometimes the road less traveled turns out to be the fastest way to get somewhere, but one must always be willing to take that risky first step.

Chapter 2

Execution First and Always

"Objectives are needed in every area where performance and results directly and vitally affect the survival and prosperity of the business."

Drucker understood from the outset that sound management was all about performing, organizing, contributing, developing, preparing, and achieving. His works are infused with dozens of words and phrases suggesting that *action* is the chief determinant of managerial success; not just any action, but responsible action that advances the objectives of the organization.

One of Drucker's key assumptions was that management is first and foremost a practice, and for a manager to excel at it, he or she must understand that it is performance that is the ultimate measure of success.

During our day together, Drucker told me what separated

the good from the fair, and the fair from the incompetent manager. Here's how he described the most capable manager:

Can hire, fire, organize … promote
Is completely accountable for results
Knows how to delegate upstairs
Makes informed decisions after thinking through the time frame
Really thinks it through and then communicates it
Is the right person for the business plan
Asks what needs to be done and sets a new priority
Ends meetings with clear assignments … most meetings end in murkiness

These tenets say a great deal about Drucker's notion of the practice of management. Managers hire, promote, and delegate (both up, and down, the hierarchy). They are strong *communicators;* they make effective decisions that help the organization, not only in the near term but for the long run. They set priorities and make sure they are executed, and when that is done, they set a new priority.

For example, Drucker told me that "Welch was the right person for the business plan." That's because Welch was the kind of leader who abandoned what didn't work (excessive management layers, bureaucracy, slow-growth businesses, autocratic leaders), and replaced them with what did (a leaner organization; high-growth, high-margin businesses; inspirational leaders; and a learning infrastructure).

Drucker also stresses the importance of removing individuals who do not execute consistently, especially at the managerial level. He argues that it is a great mistake to leave nonperformers in place to continue their incompetent ways. It is not fair to the organization or to those performers who are meeting or exceeding standards: *"It is the duty of the executive to remove ruthlessly anyone—and especially the manager who consistently fails to perform with high distinction."*

Execution Requires Abandonment

Much of the Drucker body of knowledge is aimed at making managers and "knowledge workers" more productive. Drucker coined the term *knowledge worker* in the 1960s to describe educated rather than apprenticed workers. A knowledge worker is "nonmanual," Drucker told me, "what you have to go to school to learn—what you can't learn by an apprenticeship."

The ultimate test of a manager, and the only one that counts, is one that measures accomplishment. In Drucker's view, execution isn't only accomplishing things—it's accomplishing the *right* things.

The most effective leaders know that execution and abandonment are two sides of the coin. Organizations that consistently outperform their peers are those that discard outdated strategies, products, and processes. Only through this cleansing process can an organization renew itself.

Planned abandonment is a prerequisite to consistent execution. "To call abandonment an opportunity may come as a surprise," argues Drucker. "Yet planned, purposeful abandonment of the old and of the unrewarding is a prerequisite pursuit of the new and highly promising. Above all, *abandonment is the key to innovation*—both because it frees the necessary resources and because it stimulates the search for the new that will replace the old."

Executives who fail to abandon the cash cows of yesterday, despite mounting evidence of impending failure, are guilty of poor execution. One such example is the Sony Corporation. In the 1970s Sony took the world by storm with the introduction of its cassette-playing Walkman. Sony led that market for two decades. However, long after Apple's iPod became a huge hit, Sony's leadership failed to grasp the magnitude of the threat. Even after Apple sold 60 million iPods and an incredible 1.5 billion songs from its iTunes store, Sony's Walkman division continued to offer music-only machines. As a result, Apple racked up 70 percent of all online music sales, while Sony sold only 10 percent of music players—a gut-wrenching lesson for the Japanese electronics giant that had once owned the market.

The firm failed to abandon a key fundamental belief: that hardware was the driving force in making great consumer electronics products. Apple proved it was no longer true by incorporating an easy-to-use browser on its iPod, helping to turn a good product into a colossal hit.

Barriers to Effective Execution

Managers who execute well do so because they make a habit of doing the right things while guarding against forces that threaten the company's future. The following specific factors can interfere with a manager's ability to execute consistently:

- **Failure to practice purposeful abandonment.**
  Managers should regularly review products and people to make sure they are still fulfilling their original promise.

- **Excessive bureaucracy or management layers.**
  Few things can clog an organization like excessive, oppressive management layers. If decisions get bogged down, it could be because of too much red tape and/or too many stifling layers of management.

- **The absence of clearly defined values and an operating system to share learning and ideas.**
  The most effective organizations have shared values that define the company, and they conduct meetings, reviews, and training (i.e. the operating system) to help inculcate those values throughout the firm.

- **The wrong management structure.**
  "The right structure does not guarantee results," Drucker wrote in *Managing for Results*. "But the wrong structure

aborts results. . . . Above all, structure has to be such that it highlights the results that are truly meaningful."

● **No clear strategy or one not communicated throughout the organization.**
Unless there is a clear strategy that everyone in the firm can communicate, people will not understand how their accomplishments contribute to the organization as a whole.

● **An insular culture that focuses on the wrong things and rewards the wrong behavior.**
A culture that does not encourage its people to focus on customers, the marketplace, and the "right" results will eventually falter.

On *Execution*

In 2002, former GE vice chairman (and current Jack Welch friend) Larry Bossidy teamed up with top business consultant/ author Ram Charan to pen the business megahit *Execution: The Discipline of Getting Things Done*. The timing for the book was perfect. Following in the footsteps of books such as *Reengineering the Corporation*, it became something of a movement and emerged as a phenomenon, topping best-seller lists for months and selling more than one million copies. (A million-copy business book is very rare, coming along only once every couple of years.)

Here's how the authors defined their newly found "discipline": "Execution is a specific set of behaviors and techniques that companies need to master in order to have competitive advantage. It is a discipline of its own. In big companies and small ones, it is the critical discipline for success now."

In reading the book, I could not help but feel that much of the information in the book, although dressed in different clothes, felt oddly familiar. Execution was the epicenter of most of the Drucker concepts. What to do, what to achieve, how to contribute, measure, and perform with distinction. He just didn't call it execution. As he once said, he dealt with "abstractions" and although he coined several new terms (for example, postindustrial, knowledge worker), he was more focused on creating new concepts than creating pithy names for them.

I am convinced that is one of the reasons why Drucker does not appear more often in current management textbooks. Frederick Taylor had "scientific management," France's Henri Fayol had his fourteen principles of management, and George Elton Mayo had his Human Relations movement. All of these theorists fit nicely into the syllabi of most management professors.

Drucker himself admitted early on in his career: "I have never been quite respectable in the eyes of academia."

Other management experts have their own theories for why Drucker was not more "respectable in the eyes of academia." *The Economist*'s John Micklethwait and Adrian Wooldridge have suggested that more recent scholars gained prominence by making a part of the management bookshelf their own. For example, Michael Porter's name became synonymous with strategy while Theodore Levitt was most associated with marketing. Drucker covered the entire management landscape but did not stake out any one particular niche.

When Tom Peters cowrote the megahit *In Search of Excellence* (the book that sold more than five million copies), the findings surrounding his excellent companies found their way into many best-selling books.* But with the possible exception of one of Drucker's best known concepts, management by objectives—the management tool that involves management setting goals for subordinates—he seldom garnered much attention from textbook authors.

Management by objectives (MBO) was introduced by Drucker in *The Practice of Management* (1954) and became one of his most oft-used concepts. The goal of MBO is to enhance the productivity of the organization by setting clear objectives for individuals who contribute to the strategic objectives of the firm. Key CEOs, such as Andy Grove, were faithful followers of Drucker's MBO method, which according to some "dominated strategic thinking in the postwar decades." Still, that was not enough to convince authors or business school professors of Drucker's importance.†

---

* Despite the fact that Tom Peters later admitted in *Fast Company* in November of 2001, "We faked the data."

† MBO lost its luster in the early 1980s, criticized because it was more top down than bottom up, more fitting for a command-and-control, hierarchical company.

According to both Tom Peters and management expert James O'Toole, despite the large number of books Drucker wrote, finding a Drucker book in an MBA program is rare indeed. Peters said he had not been assigned a single Drucker book while getting two advanced business degrees, including an MBA at Stanford. O'Toole took it one step further when he said, "Peter would never have gotten tenure in a major business school."

However, none of these issues lessen his contributions: he may not have come up with neat terms for his ideas, but he was still first to articulate the thoughts behind them.

To illustrate the point, see the two excerpts below, which have been compiled from two books written half a century apart. Take a close look not only at the words, but the meaning behind them. Is there really a difference between the concepts behind Bossidy and Charan's *Execution* and Drucker's *The Practice of Management*? Or is this a question of semantics? Or is it simply another instance of Drucker's getting there first and then others following many years later, quite independently of the management pioneer? Please note that these brief excerpts are not continuous thoughts—they are excerpted from different parts of each of the two books:

Execution by the Book, 2002

"Execution is not just tactics—it is a discipline and a system. It has to be built into the company's strategy, its goals, its culture. And the leader of the organization must be deeply involved in it. He cannot delegate its substance. Many business leaders spend vast amounts of time learning and promulgating the latest management techniques [Ram Charan, page 6]. When I see companies that don't execute, the chances are that they don't measure, don't reward, and don't promote people who know how to get things done" [Larry Bossidy, page 73].

[Source: Bossidy/Charan, *Execution*, Crown Business, 2002]

And from Drucker's *The Practice of Management*:

"Management must always, in every decision and action, put economic performance first. It can only justify its existence and its authority by the economic results it produces. . . . And yet the ultimate test of management is business performance. . . . To be able to control his performance a manager needs to know more than what his goals are. He must be able to measure his performance and results against the goal. Objectives are needed in every area where performance and results directly and vitally affect the survival and prosperity of the business."

[Source: Drucker, *The Practice of Management*, Harper & Row, 1954, pages 7–8, 9–10, 131]

Chapter 3

Broken Washroom Doors

"Every business has its 'broken washroom doors,' its misdirections, its policies, procedures and methods that emphasize and reward wrong behavior, penalize or inhibit right behavior."

uring our day together it was clear that Drucker was intensely focused on what managers did right, what they did wrong, what worked, and what didn't. He was even more interested in the "whys" behind organizational success and failure. While he wolfed down his lunch (he ate faster than he did anything else), he delivered a lecture on the greatest problems facing one particular segment of society. He spoke of nonprofit organizations as examples that had gotten it wrong more often than they had gotten it right, and what all managers could learn from their mistakes.

"Few people realize the competition for nonprofit money is much more severe than the competition for goods in the marketplace," Drucker asserted. "That's really severe competition. In many nonprofits, the lack of results only means that you should do more of it."

Drucker said the problem of having people in positions where they do the least amount of good exists everywhere, but it is more rampant in hospitals, churches, and other nonprofits than in corporations.

To raise productivity in most any organization managers should regularly assess their key people, their strengths, and the results they achieve. Then they should ask themselves: Do we have the right people in the right jobs, where they can make the greatest contributions? Are the jobs the right ones, meaning do we have people performing tasks that even if achieved do not add value to the organization? What changes in people, jobs, and job functions can we make that will yield greater results?

Broken Compensation Systems

By the mid-1980s, Drucker had grown disgusted with corporate America. The salaries of chief executives were "totally out of control," he argued. CEOs were being paid millions in salary and stock options regardless of how their companies performed, while laying off tens of thousands of workers.

Drucker felt stock options were shortsighted and rewarded the wrong outcomes, since they gave managers an incentive to manage for today while sacrificing tomorrow. He said a stock's performance should not be a criterion in deciding on CEO compensation.

He said it was obscene for CEOs to be paid hundreds of times that of the typical worker, while in Japan the typical CEO was being paid no more than forty times the average worker. As a result, Drucker began to condemn the very institutions he had written about for forty years, which explains why he had turned his attention to nonprofits. Drucker had been a consultant to nonprofit organizations for years, but his revulsion for the avarice of C-level executives proved to be the tipping point.

Corporate America was in a state of transition in the 1980s. During the prior decade, companies had hunkered down, attempting to regain their edge in the years following a fierce bear stock market, multiple recessions, an oil embargo, and sky-high interest rates that hovered around 20 percent.

However, in the 1980s, companies like General Electric went on the offensive. Determined to grow the bottom line at any cost, companies restructured—eliminating layers of management and laying off unprecedented numbers of workers.

In addition, multibillion-dollar acquisitions, many of them hostile, were a big part of the problem, asserted Drucker. They usually did more harm than good to the companies involved. Worst of all, CEO pay continued to skyrocket while workers were being eliminated in record numbers. Between 1970 and 1990, CEO pay increased by roughly 400 percent while the pay of average workers barely budged when adjusted for inflation. This made absolutely no sense to Drucker, who was the first to view workers as a company's greatest asset—not a cost—as had been the prevailing wisdom before him.

All of this greed was a stinging indictment of the Jeffersonian ideal that Drucker had espoused since his first business book: "This is morally and socially unforgivable," wrote Ducker, who felt that a CEO's pay should be capped at about twenty times the average worker. "We will pay a heavy price for it," he cautioned, and went further by labeling these egregious practices "the final failure of corporate capitalism." In Drucker's view, the corporation itself had become something of a "broken washroom door."

Get the 80 and the 20 Right

Drucker, never one afraid to follow his gut, turned his full attention to nonprofits. Churches, universities and other schools, health and community services, charitable and service groups—even the Girl Scouts—all became enthusiastic Drucker clients. "I did a fair amount of consulting work on innovation with colleges and universities and churches," Drucker told me.

However, it was neither church nor university that posed the greatest management challenge. According to Drucker, the institution that has the most broken washroom doors is the hospital: "Let me say the most difficult management job is the hospital."

Drucker then explained that hospitals only work well on patients facing life-threatening illnesses: "Hospitals don't like people who aren't seriously sick," he said. He added that if an old woman goes into cardiac arrest at three in the morning, the floor nurse gets a team to work on her within minutes. But other than dealing with life-threatening emergencies, hospitals are "totally disorganized."

"Hospitals don't like the people who aren't seriously sick" is another classic Druckerism. The majority of people kept waiting in a hospital emergency room with a minor injury know that Drucker is on the mark. "Hospitals like crises. They are organized for crises, but 80 percent of the patients are not crises … they do very poorly."

Drucker's 80 percent doctrine regarding hospitals forces us to look at business in a different way. The 80/20 principle—80 percent of a company's business comes from 20 percent of its customers—is a well-worn, well-known truism. However, in reframing the 80/20 principle from a different perspective— how a business is organized for the minority of its customers— Drucker forces us to rethink some of the basic assumptions and strategies upon which our businesses are based.

One of the keys is to take nothing for granted. For example, there are times when paying attention to the smaller, untapped part of a market can reap huge dividends. Drucker urged managers to pay close attention, not only to a firm's customers but to its noncustomers.

One example of a contemporary company that did this well is the weight loss company NutriSystem. It floundered in the

1990s, and changed its name twice before sharpening its strategic focus in the early 2000s. In 2006, it increased revenues by 167 percent (to $568 million), and operating income and net income by roughly 300 percent.

It did it by focusing on a segment of the weight loss market ignored by its peers—men—even though men constitute only a fifth of the market. Its CEO proclaimed that it had proved that the men's weight loss market, long neglected by commercial weight loss companies, can become a large opportunity for NutriSystem. The company, however, did not ignore its core customers (women).

Unlike most institutions, hospitals must be designed and organized for the 20 percent. They have no choice. They are the last line of defense for serious illness and trauma. However, the hospital example is an extreme one. The vast majority of organizations are not as constrained. Senior managers can, and should, create organizations that best serve the needs of the majority of their current customers, or core, unless they are expecting some dramatic shift in the business landscape (for example, new technologies, competitors) or customer base (for example, shifting demographics). However, as the NutriSystem example proved, there are opportunities and potential windfalls to be had for those organizations that can bring in significant numbers of noncustomers as well.

Protecting Washroom Doors

There are a number of things a manager can do to minimize mishaps, bad policies, unsound methods, and habits that inhibit poor performance:

- **Make sure your best people are placed where they can make the greatest contributions** (for example, put strength on strength).

- **Write down your priorities, but no more than two,** and make sure that your people are also focused on the right priorities. Drucker asserted he never knew a manager who could handle more than two priorities at a time.

- **Maintain an outside-in perspective** by ensuring that all managers spend time with customers in the marketplace, the only place results exist (see next chapter for much more on this topic).

- **Review systems, processes, and policies** and abandon any that add to bureaucracy and diminish productivity.

- **Review compensation systems** to make sure you are rewarding outcomes that can actually move the needle.

Mission Statements Prevent Dysfunction

Drucker wrote early on that defining a business is important, but never easy. One of the complicating factors can be traced back to his most fundamental law of business: *"Only a customer can define business purpose."* Let's revisit Drucker's hospital example a final time to examine this in depth.

Drucker once described how he had worked with a team of hospital administrators to create a mission statement for their emergency room. That might seem like a relatively simple task, but it wasn't. He had no use for generalities, such as "Our mission is health care," the most common mission statement of most hospitals. That is the wrong definition, asserted Drucker. "The hospital is not a health care provider; the hospital takes care of *illness*," he argued.

"Mission statements have to be operational; otherwise it's merely good intentions." To Drucker, a better statement for the hospital emergency room is "giving assurance to the afflicted." Although many hospital administrators thought that definition was too general and "awfully obvious," Drucker thought it right on target, since it acknowledges the 80 percent as well as the 20 percent.

After all, he reasoned, giving assurance is what the emergency room does for the vast majority of people who visit. " 'Your son has a high fever but he will be all right,' says the emergency room doctor after examining a young boy. 'Your mother has a serious rash but it is not life threatening.' 'Your sister's ankle is sprained; go home and put ice on it.' Less than 20 percent of patients possess serious maladies that require immediate medical attention." Drucker's focus was always on the real problem and not the distractions that had the potential to sidetrack even the best-intentioned managers.

Drucker said the manager's job is to try to convert "the organization's mission statement into specifics." Only specific mission statements tell the rank and file what they need to contribute for the organization to reach its objectives.

During lunch Drucker expanded his hospital example to reinforce other key points, such as how even a "poor" organization can be good at something once the mission is clearly defined: even a poor hospital is very good in a crisis, and that's what they love, that's what they are there for. Hospitals love emergencies—they thrive on crisis.

Drucker also explained how an organization's mission plays a pivotal role in determining the type of talent it will attract. For example, the type of nurse who chooses to work in a an emergency room is completely different from the nurse who works in a doctor's office: "If you don't want to be a crisis nurse, you work in a doctor's office, where there are no crises [and] the work is much easier." Drucker explained that when a patient goes into convulsions in the middle of the night and calls his doctor, the physician instructs the patient to go the emergency room. "Then the hospital takes over, not the doctor's nurse."

Broken Doors in the Publishing Business

Let's consider one more example of how an organization that focuses on the wrong things becomes dysfunctional. This example comes from a relatively small industry, the book-publishing business. Drucker told me with some irony that although his name, Drucker, means "printer," he has never been more wrong about predicting the future of a business. Throughout his career, he said that he had gotten more things wrong about publishing than any other industry.

Perhaps that is because book publishing is unique in that its products come not from assembly lines, but from the hearts, minds, and creativity of its authors. Another important factor is how the author's talents match with countless other variables that are important to the reader at the time of publication. However, book publishing does resemble many other businesses in that the vast majority of its revenues (probably 90 percent) come from a small percentage of its products (say 10 percent). Also, books are not market tested before they are published.

Instead of one focused brand, a typical large publisher is working with more than 100 new titles per publishing season. Nabisco would never come out with, say, 100 new types of cookies every spring, summer, and fall. Coke wouldn't come out with 150 new beverages. Books are one of the few consumer products *not* treated like consumer products.

However, because the performance of many popular books

is a surprise—both to the upside and downside—publishers have no way to weed out the "dogs" before they are published. However, it is what happens *after* a book is published that reveals one of the real broken washroom doors in the system.

Many authors whose books have failed, that is, the writers who produce the worst-performing products, often consume much of the organization's resources. Frustrated authors sometimes bombard the publisher with complaints, phone calls, e-mails, and letters. Many authors take their arguments to the very top of the organization. When that happens, the organization goes into overdrive to stop the bleeding and "fix" the problem.

When that irate letter is sent down the hierarchy, often from the president's or CEO's office, editors and marketing managers are forced to drop everything to mollify its author. Few authors understand that once a book has failed it has failed for good. No amount of advertising or promotion can save it. With more than 175,000 books published each year in the United States it is of little wonder that the majority fail.

That's just one example. How many businesses and corporations have similar examples? According to Drucker, all companies have a tendency to focus on the wrong things at one time or another: "Every business has its 'broken washroom doors,' its misdirections, its policies, procedures and methods that emphasize and reward wrong behavior, penalize or inhibit right behavior."

To make sure broken washroom doors do not take over a company, senior managers must be certain that the organization, its people, and its systems, are focused on those products, offerings, and customers that deliver the lion's share of the business. And highly capable people must be assigned to work on the cash cows of tomorrow. One way to achieve this is to assign one or more small teams a specific assignment, product, or idea that has the potential to become a significant part of the company's future. That's one of the ways an organization can build innovation into the fabric of the company. However, organizations must always make sure that the decisions they make benefit the firm in both the near future and in the long run. And they must be sure not to neglect their core businesses and customers, or they might not have a future to safeguard.

Broken Washroom Doors

To make sure that broken washroom doors do not derail a company, managers must assess their direct reports on a regular basis so that people are placed where they can make the greatest difference. In addition, reviews of systems and processes should occur on a regular basis to rid the organization of any that no longer make sense. Also, make sure that everyone in the organization can articulate its mission. Only specific mission statements tell the company's employees what they need to contribute for the organization to attain its objectives. Last, to make sure they do not miss out on opportunities, managers must strive to convert some customers into noncustomers. This means not being sidetracked or distracted by "broken doors" that do nothing but eat away at managers' time and resources (as we saw in the publishing example).

Chapter 4

Outside-In

> "The executive is within an organization . . . he sees the outside only through thick and distorting lenses, if at all. What goes on outside is usually not even known firsthand. It is received through an organizational filter of reports."

In recent years much has been written about the importance of maintaining an "outside-in" perspective: seeing one's organization through the eyes of a customer, supplier, or other more objective outsider.

That topic was important enough to capture the attention of several high-profile authors and academics. Noel Tichy (who headed GE's Crotonville management training facility in the mid-1980s) and überconsultant Ram Charan tackled the subject in their critically acclaimed book *Every Business Is a Growth Business* (2000). More recently, an MIT author, Barbara Bund, devoted an entire book to the topic in *The Outside-In Corpora-tion*.

As we have seen with so many other important topics, Peter Drucker was the intellectual father of the outside-in corporation.

Outside-in is classic Drucker. Developing an outside-in perspective means abandoning yesterday's perspective. It means embracing a new reality: seeing your organization from the customer's vantage point. And an organization is not a manager's ally in this effort.

Drucker was the first management writer to write that an organization, by its very nature, has the potential to imprison a manager, diminish his or her field of vision, and destroy a leader's effectiveness. However, he did not come to that conclusion overnight. There was an evolution to his thinking.

First, there was what I call Drucker's Law, which he described in his 1954 watershed book *The Practice of Management*: *"There is only one valid definition of business purpose: to create a customer."* This emerged as Drucker's most heralded management principle. He once mused that its appeal was due to its simplicity, because it had "only one moving part." Drucker would build on that concept in two future books by describing the realities and limitations that affect every manager.

Eight Realities for Every Manager

In his 1964 book, *Managing for Results*, a book Drucker calls a "what to do book," he advances his discussion of outside-in.

He also argues that many managers get caught up in a "rat race" existence in which all they have time to do is respond to "whatever the mail boy dumps in their in-tray" (today's equivalent of the e-mail in-box, and the ultimate inside-out behavior). That type of passive management—let's call it management by in-basket (my term, not Drucker's)—is a prescription for failure. However, Drucker explains why management by in-basket is a common trap that trips up the vast majority of managers.

He starts by laying out eight realities of business that all managers must deal with in order to maximize the company's performance. These realities constitute "the fundamentals and constants of the outside environment, the things the business executive has to consider as givens, as constraints and challenges." How an organization deals with these realities determines its fate. Those that can turn these constraints into opportunities will achieve superior results over the long run. Here is a quick summary of Drucker's eight business realities:

- **Results and resources exist outside the business.**
  Time and again Drucker stressed that there are no profits within an organization, only cost centers. What most call profit centers are really cost centers, he said. Results never depend on anyone within the company but, instead, on customers in the marketplace. "It is always somebody outside who decides whether the efforts of a business become economic results or whether they become so much waste and scrap," argued Drucker.

- **Results are achieved by exploiting opportunities, not solving problems.**
  Solving problems can only return the organization to its prior status quo. To achieve results managers must exploit opportunities. However, in most organizations, its best people spend too much time putting out fires rather than searching for new opportunities that can become tomorrow's cash cows.

- **To obtain results, resources must be allocated to opportunities.**
  Too many managers make the mistake of throwing away resources by allocating them to fixing problems. "Maximization of opportunities is a meaningful, indeed a precise, definition of the entrepreneurial job. It implies that effectiveness rather than efficiency is essential to business. The key is not how to do things right but to do the right things," declared Drucker.

- **The most meaningful results go to market leaders.**
  "Profits are the rewards for making a unique, or at least a distinct contribution ... something the market accepts as value," asserts Drucker. Size does not determine leadership. The biggest rewards do not necessarily go to the biggest companies. "A company which wants economic results has to have leadership in *something* of real value to a customer or market," wrote Drucker. "It may be in one

narrow but important aspect of the product line, it may be in its service, it may be in its distribution, or it may be in the ability to convert ideas into saleable products . . . speedily and at a low cost."

● **Leadership, however, is short-lived and not likely to last.**
Market leadership is temporary. "Business tends to shift from leadership to mediocrity," wrote Drucker. "It is the manager's job to reverse that trend and to ensure that resources go to the areas that offer the greatest chance of success and away from problem areas. "Managers must reverse the trend toward mediocrity by providing new energy and a new direction."

● **What exists is getting old.**
Drucker explains that managers "spend more of their time trying to unmake the past than anything else." Today's winning products are a part of yesterday. Even the best managers fall into the trap of working on yesterday. The most effective executives understand that their decisions and actions, once incorporated into the business, are made obsolete by events or changing conditions. "Any human decision or action starts to get old the moment it has been made," wrote Drucker. "Just as generals tend to prepare for the last war, businessmen always tend to react in terms of the last boom or of the last depression."

● **What exists is likely to be misallocated.**

Here Drucker invokes the 80/20 rule but says that it is more like 90/10. That is, the first 10 percent of effort in a firm produces 90 percent of the results. This is true with products, customers, even salespeople (the top 10 percent of salespeople produce 90 percent of the results). The key, then, is to make sure that the best in your company—whether people or physical resources—are allocated to projects or products that have the potential to deliver the lion's share of tomorrow's business.

● **To achieve the greatest economic results, concentrate.**

Companies must avoid the temptation to dabble in many things. Instead, they must focus their efforts on just a few products, services, customers, markets, et cetera. Drucker contends that no other rule of business is violated as often as the principle of concentration. Similarly, when cutting costs, managers tend to cut a little bit off of everything (including muscle), rather than cutting off fat. This approach can quickly derail a company. Instead, managers need to be far more strategic by figuring out which areas should not be touched and which can be cut far more liberally without harming the fundamentals of the business.

Three years later, in *The Effective Executive*, Drucker added to his "there are no results within the organization" doctrine.

Drucker suggested that far too many organizations become shortsighted and insular, because they do not spend enough time in the marketplace, which he called *"the only place that matters."*

This is why a myopic, inward point of view (for example, inside-out) does nothing to help managers understand the company's most important constituency. But developing an outside-in perspective is not a simple exercise; it is complicated by several other "inescapable realities" of organizational life.

These realities, when combined with the eight realities Drucker described in *Managing for Results*, provide a complete picture of the obstacles that confront every manager every day. These timeless observations are as useful today as when Drucker first wrote of them more than four decades ago.

More Management Realities

One reality is that an executive's time belongs to *everybody else*. That is, managers are captives of their own organizations. They have bosses, boards, direct reports, presentations, budgets, and human resource problems to deal with.

There are so many distractions to sop up an executive's time that a manager's time can never be called her own. And the more senior the manager, the less control she has over her own time. "Captive" executives have a hard time seeing past their own in-basket, never mind getting a clear view of the marketplace.

Another reality, argues Drucker, is that "the executive is

within an organization . . . He sees the outside only through thick and distorting lenses, if at all. What goes on outside is usually not even known firsthand. It is received through an organizational filter of reports."

This is why it is so critical for managers to develop an outside-in perspective, to neutralize the effects of the claustrophobic realities of an organization.

Those two realities—that a manager's time is not her own and the fact that she sees the marketplace only through thick and distorting lenses—makes developing an outside-in perspective a key management challenge. Drucker also made the point that the chief executive is the crucial connection between inside and outside. While this lesson may not seem particularly difficult, it took one of the era's most accomplished CEOs many years before he grasped the full import of outside-in.

Welch's Big Idea

Jack Welch once told a New York audience, "*Outside-in is a big idea. We've been inside-out for over a hundred years. Forcing everything around the outside-in view will change the game.*" Welch made those comments in 1999 to a diverse audience at the 92nd Street Y in Manhattan, almost two decades after he became GE's chairman.

Many great companies have fallen from grace because their top managers have failed to maintain the right perspective, or failed to recognize that some key market dynamic changed the reality of their operating environment.

IBM, for example, was in a death spiral when its board hired RJR Nabisco's CEO to turn the company around. Snack food king Lou Gerstner was the last person anyone expected to fix a broken Big Blue. In 1993, the company had chalked up some $8 billion in red ink. Gerstner quickly figured out that the company had become so large and bureaucratic that it had lost touch with its customers. The stock had fallen below $15 for the first time since the 1980s and its outlook was bleak.

Gerstner turned out to be the right guy at the right time for IBM. He told me for a previous book (*What the Best CEOs Know*) "that a big part of what I had to do was get the company refocused on the marketplace as the only valid measure of success." Gerstner added, "I started by telling virtually every audience ... that there was a customer running IBM, and that we were going to rebuild the company from the customer back. Those are pretty simple statements, but hugely important in reshaping the mindset."

Reshaping mind-sets is a big part of what Drucker is all about. Abandoning an outdated mind-set for one that fits a new reality is classic Drucker.

That's what Gerstner did after IBM's arrogance caused it to miss the personal computing revolution. That outside-in mindset helped reinvent the company and help it turn an $8 billion *loss* into a $5 billion *gain* within five years.

GE provides one more example of how focusing on customers and the marketplace can make a huge difference in helping companies to succeed. This involved Jack Welch's signature strategy of Six Sigma—the quality initiative that helps organizations reduce the number of defects or mistakes to fewer than 3.4 per million. Welch implemented the companywide program with more vigor than any other initiative at GE.

Welch had watched as managers inside the company celebrated the success of GE's Six Sigma quality initiatives, at precisely the time customers were complaining that things were not getting better. In Drucker's parlance, the thick walls of the company had distorted the view of his managers. That's when Welch threw a fit at his annual senior managers' meeting, letting everyone know that things had to change. Only then did he really get the lesson of outside-in.

The Outside-In Retailer

Another company that lives by Drucker's outside-in imperative is Tesco PLC, the UK's largest grocer/retailer and the world's fourth largest retailer (only Wal-Mart, Home Depot, and France's Carrefour Group are larger). This innovative and highly successful company has been reinvented by starting with the customer and working its way back to the company.

One of the company's strategies has been to diversify its offerings by selling services not typically offered by supermarkets, such as banking and financial services. It is now one of the fastest-growing financial services companies in Europe.

To reinvent the company, management started with its mission. It is engraved on a plaque that greets all who enter its Cheshunt, England, headquarters: CREATE VALUE FOR CUSTOMERS TO EARN THEIR LIFETIME LOYALTY (note that it is customer value—not shareholder value—that is the primary concern of management, proving the adage "Take care of the customers and the profits will follow").

The firm's values reinforce the company's mission. The value that tops Tesco's list is to "understand customers better than anyone."

Given its current success, it may be hard to believe that not long ago Tesco was a second-rate company, known for poor customer service and for copying competitors. It lost 1 to 2 percent of market share each year in the early 1990s.

To turn things around, the company did not make one move, but many, instituted over several years. Its managers called the company's effort "bricks in the wall," meaning that the firm's success was due to many "incremental," customer-focused changes rather than any one sweeping alteration.

One important move was the creation of a management program dubbed TWIST, or Tesco Week in Store Together. In the TWIST program, managers work in a Tesco store performing some function designed to give that manager greater understanding of the customer and how his or her job fits into the larger scheme of things. The logistics/IT manager, for example, stocks store shelves. The CEO waits on customers at a cash register.

There were several other moves that added up to greater customer satisfaction and loyalty. In 1993, it created a line of lower-priced value products. This "value" line was introduced under a separate label, known as "own label" in Britain. In 1994, the firm brought "one in front" to reality, a plan that calls for its stores to open up new checkout lines if any checkout line has more than two customers waiting.

In 1995, it brought out its now signature Clubcard program, which returns 1 percent of a customer's purchase in a rebate program. That program, one of the most successful loyalty efforts ever launched, inspired an entire book, titled *Scoring Points: How Tesco Continues to Win Customer Loyalty*.

That explains how Tesco emerged as the UK's number one retailer, locking up more than 30 percent of the grocery market. The firm also profitably expanded into central Europe and Asia.

It is also a company that recognizes the cultural differences of its customers. The products it sells outside of Britain are tailored to the needs of locals in each of the markets it serves.

Tesco's CEO, Sir Terry Leahy, garnered a reputation as one of the world's premier CEOs and the attention of the international press. The *Economist* wrote of Leahy that he does "not change as much as a lightbulb without poring over customer surveys and sales data first." Peter Drucker would have liked the way Terry Leahy does business.

Master the Habits of Outside-In

What can a manager do to overcome the "thick and distorting lenses" Drucker describes at the outset of this chapter? What can one do to develop an outside-in perspective? Consider the following:

- **Go where the customers are.**

  Take a page from Tesco's TWIST program by having your people work directly with customers. Attend meetings, conferences, and any other events or gatherings that bring you face-to-face with your customers. And don't forget noncustomers, people who do not currently buy your offerings but may do so in the future.

- **Invite customers and suppliers to meet with your people.**

  There's no substitute for direct dialogue. The more contact your people have with the company's most important constituents, the more they will learn about their needs and preferences.

● **Use technology to enhance customer satisfaction.**
Wal-Mart uses sophisticated computer and satellite technology to get information flowing between stores, ware-
houses, and the home office. This technology lets them
know precisely what has been purchased so they can re-
stock shelves daily and never be out of key items (for example, Pampers). Tesco uses heat sensors to identify
bottlenecks and congestion in its stores (the same technology that is used to detect survivors in fallen buildings). This technology improves flow around its stores so
that it may better serve its customers.

● **Spend two to four hours each week on competitive
Web sites, in stores, and wherever your competitors
are.**
If your firm does a substantial amount of its business online, then its marketplace is on the Web. Make sure your
people know what your competitors are up to so that you
can stay one step ahead or counter their latest competitive threats.

Outside-In

There was an evolution to Drucker's thinking that led to his outside-in imperative. First there was Drucker's Law: "There is only one valid definition of business purpose: to create a customer." Then he described his eight business principles, which gave a broader view of why an outside-in perspective is so critical to success. These principles included a discussion of how results only happen on the outside, how resources must go to opportunities and not problems, and how the most efficient companies focus on the smallest number of offerings. Later he added two more realities that affect a manager's ability to develop an outside-in perspective: first, an executive is a captive of the organization, meaning that his time is not his own. Also, a manager sees the marketplace through thick and distorting lenses—if at all. This means that a manager must be proactive in making sure that he or she gets an unfiltered view of the marketplace by getting as close as possible to customers. One good model for this is the UK retailer Tesco and its TWIST program. TWIST stands for Tesco Week in Store Together, in which senior managers work for a full week at the store level to give them a greater understanding of the inner workings of the business; more important, they get an up close, unfettered view of the customer.

Chapter 5

When Naturals Run Out

"What a manager does can be analyzed systematically. What a manager has to be able to do can be learned. . . . But one quality cannot be learned, one qualification that the manager cannot acquire but must bring with him. It is not genius; it is character."

Drucker spent a good deal of time talking about "naturals"—those talented individuals who are perceived as born managers. Naturals set the right priorities, inspire others, and know how to make life-and-death decisions. Naturals do not micromanage people to death. They understand intuitively that autocratic leaders are not effective and are a part of yesterday.

They know that intimidation is stifling and counterproductive, particularly when it comes to creativity. They are a confident bunch, and trust their own ability to make the tough decisions. They set the right priorities, execute consistently—even in tough times—and get promoted more quickly, and more often, than their peers.

This chapter will examine naturals—first in the same historical context Drucker described them to me—then will fast-forward to detail some of the key Drucker lessons associated with these talented A-level managers.

The Birth of the Modern Corporation

Drucker's selection of topics that December day gave me the impression that he saw me as his biographer, even though I had told him from day one that I had no plans to write his biography. My goal, as I explained to Drucker, was to shine the light on his best management ideas and show how they can be applied in today's turbulent global marketplace. Still, that did not stop him from regaling me with story after story from his past. Although we hardly discussed the items we had agreed to in advance, I now know he gave me more than I asked for. He provided a rare glimpse into his life and thinking, including stories and lessons that he had not spoken of before, or after.

Not long after we began it became clear that Drucker was determined to place his contributions in a larger context. He felt the best way to achieve that was to take me back to the birth of the modern-day corporation—how and when it was created, structured, et cetera. He also went to great lengths to credit his "forebears," those who had paved the way for what he would later create (see chapter 6 for more on the business pioneers Drucker admired most).

He began by tracing the large corporation back to the 1870s. He explained that really large corporations came after the Civil War. Interestingly enough, large corporations were created simultaneously in the United States, Germany, Japan, and the United Kingdom. France did not develop as quickly. Drucker said France held on to "family companies longer than any of the major powers."

"There have been managers all through the ages, but they were very few and far between," continued Drucker. Before the advent of the large corporation, the most capable members of the family managed the family business. Drucker called the best of these naturals. "But suddenly, you could no longer depend on the supply of naturals," said Drucker. "You could only depend on the supply of naturals when the demand is low. But when you need large numbers of talented managers, you have to convert management into something that can be learned or taught. And that's what I did." By establishing management as a discipline, he provided the much-needed tools that could transform non-naturals into competent managers.

Drucker's books were used to educate thousands of managers who were needed as corporations exploded in number and size during the post–World War II management boom. His publication of *The Practice of Management* in 1954 was a seminal event, as it was regarded as the best how-to-manage manual of the modern era. For example, in 1956, when David Packard (of Hewlett-Packard) set out to draw up the goals for his company, he turned to Drucker's *The Practice of Management*, so asserts Jim Collins, author of *Good to Great*. Collins added that *Practice* "stands as perhaps the most important management book ever written." That's high praise indeed from the author of one of the best-selling business books in history.

The Atlantic Monthly's senior editor and NPR commentator Jack Beatty, author of the 1998 book *The World According to Drucker*, agrees with Collins. Here is how Beatty, who interviewed Drucker at length, viewed the significance of *The Practice of Management*: "On or about November 6, 1954, Peter Drucker invented management. His timing was felicitous: the management boom of the 1950s and 1960s was set to go off, yet there was no book to herald it, no book to explain management to managers, no book to establish management as among the major social innovations of the twentieth century. Drucker would supply the lack."

When I asked Drucker about that reference—about how Beatty claimed he invented management in 1954—he looked genuinely amused and said that Beatty "must know something that I do not." To this day I don't know if Drucker was sticking to the humble "I did not invent management" script he had read from for years, or just wanted to deflect the subject. Few would dispute, however, that Drucker was the right thinker—and the right writer—at the right time.

In the five decades that followed *Practice*, he affected millions of leaders and aspiring leaders. This incredible list included the heads of such institutions as GM, Ford, and The World Bank. It has also been reported that he advised Margaret Thatcher to privatize the British mining industry.

Jim Collins described Drucker's direct influence on the "visionary" companies he wrote about: "In our research for the book *Built to Last*, Jerry Porras and I came across a number of great companies whose leaders had been shaped by Drucker's writings, including Merck, Procter & Gamble, Ford, General Electric, and Motorola. Multiply this impact across thousands of organizations of all types from police departments to symphony orchestras to government agencies and business corporations and it is hard to escape the conclusion that Drucker is one of the most influential individuals of the twentieth century." For the record, the eighteen visionary firms in *Built to Last* outperformed the overall stock market by a factor of fifteen in that book's extensive multiyear study.

Best-selling author and *BusinessWeek* executive editor John Byrne, who interviewed Drucker many times over more than twenty years, wrote this of the management pioneer in his *BusinessWeek* cover story entitled "The Man Who Invented Management": "The story of Peter Drucker is the story of management itself. It's the story of the rise of the modern corporation and the managers who organize work. Without his analysis it's almost impossible to imagine the rise of dispersed, globe-spanning corporations."

Drucker's Six Most Important Books

Drucker told me what he felt were his six most important books. The first two were no surprise, but one or two of the others were.

Concept of the Corporation (1946)
The Practice of Management (1954)
Managing for Results (1964)
The Effective Executive (1966)
The Age of Discontinuity (1969)
Innovation and Entrepreneurship (1985)

Middle Managers and the Knowledge Society

I was very conscious of time when I was with Drucker, knowing that our hours together were limited. The morning flew by and just after noon I helped him into the rental car and drove him to his favorite Italian restaurant in downtown Claremont.

Drucker had already given me a partial history lesson on the origin of large corporations, but I wanted to know how things evolved from there. He said, "The company that most management books took for granted, until very recently, was the corporation of 1918." Corporations from that period, said Drucker, "had a handful of people at the top, and a large, undifferentiated mass of unskilled or semiskilled people below." The middle management that we know of today did not exist then, he told me. "Middle management is a postwar . . . not true," said

Drucker, stopping himself in midstream, "but middle management before World War II was very thin."

He said that many companies went on with that lopsided (my word, not his) structure for years: "Actually, even the companies I first knew in this country still had first line supervisors reporting directly to top management. I am thinking of manufacturing companies . . . Remington, for instance, in Connecticut," he said.

Having spent most of my years as a middle manager, I found it hard to imagine companies without them. That prompted me to ask Drucker how middle managers came into being. He said DuPont was the first company to have them, or at least one of the earliest (founded in 1802, it made only black powder, gunpowder, until 1880). At DuPont, as with other family businesses, only family members were allowed to get into top management, Drucker explained.

He then turned it around and asked me, "What do you do with those able workers who were not family?" You give them middle management jobs, I answered. "Right, *Du Pont invented middle management jobs just to keep them.*" The Du Pont whom Drucker was talking about was Pierre S. du Pont (1870–1954), who served as president of the diversified company from 1915 to 1919.

Later, in 1920, Pierre du Pont invested heavily in GM, which at the time faced bankruptcy, and worked with Alfred Sloan to create a decentralized management structure at the struggling automobile company.

Both du Pont and Sloan were naturals, but they both headed organizations that would require larger and larger numbers of trained managers as their organizations ballooned in size. Drucker explained that World War II changed everything, due in large part to the G. I. Bill, the bill that promised that the U.S. government would pay for college and offer business loans to all returning servicemen: "The G. I. Bill of Rights changed American society because it meant that enormous numbers of people who would never have thought of going to college went to college," said Drucker. "And once you have been to college you don't . . . want to be a blue-collar worker on the plant floor. The supply created the knowledge society, not the demand," Drucker reported.

With millions of additional educated workers entering the workforce there was never a greater need for tools to help people learn the intricacies of becoming a manager. That's why Drucker's timing was so fortuitous.

The G. I. Bill was signed by Franklin Roosevelt in 1944. By the time the bill ended in 1956 almost half of the 16 million returning World War II veterans (7.8 million) had attended college or other forms of formal education. This had the effect of adding millions of educated "knowledge workers" to the workforce.

Drucker's *Concept of the Corporation* was published in 1946 and *The Practice of Management* in 1954. The former extolled the virtues of a decentralized management structure (DuPont, GM, Sears, and GE were the first to decentralize, before 1929), while the latter was a detailed playbook that showed people who never managed anything how to define a business, manage people, and set priorities.

Anatomy of a Natural

To understand what Drucker meant by the term *natural* we can examine some of what he told me during our interview. When discussing his own abilities, he made it quite clear that while he was an effective management author, he never *practiced* it. "I have no business experience, basically" became his mantra. He added that as a consultant he did not follow his own advice: "Like any consultant, don't do as I do, do as I tell you to do." However, while he didn't do any of the things he advised other people to do, he had written close to three dozen books over sixty years, most of them books on management or books on society (except for two novels and an autobiography).

While it was clear that he was a prolific management writer, he continued to make it clear that he did not have the DNA of a leader. That paradox was very much on his mind the day we met, which explains why he described himself as follows:

"I cannot manage people."

"I am a loner."

"I can neither hire people nor fire people."

"I am totally hopeless."

In stark contrast, here is how he described the born manager he had spoken of after observing her in action for many years. This particular individual was an attorney:

"She can place people."
"She can hire or fire people without becoming emotionally upset."
"She decides priorities."

He added that this individual was promoted more quickly than her contemporaries: "In every law firm she joined she soon was the managing partner," he said.

A Brief Primer on "Making" Naturals

It is worth noting that the assumption of this chapter—making new naturals—presents yet another paradox. If one is a natural, or a born manager, how can we create new ones? The answer lies as much in the *selection* of managers as it does in their training, development, and experience gained on the job. Let's delve deeper into Drucker's idea of a born manager:

Drucker's born managers can *"place people."*
Translation: They have an intuitive sense about putting people in positions where they can make the greatest contribution. This is often more difficult than it sounds, particularly because Drucker made it clear that management is a *social* discipline.

Placing people involves not only matching strength on strength, but also putting them in units or departments where personality clashes and potential turf battles are minimized.

"She can hire or fire people without becoming emotionally upset."

This can be tougher to detect in the interviewing process. One idea to help you detect the real deal is to devise a scenario and ask what that applicant would do when facing that particular set of circumstances. For example, you might paint a bleak picture of a fictional employee with questionable abilities, and ask the prospective manager how he or she might deal with that individual. Another more direct approach is to simply ask his or her previous boss how the applicant handled hiring and firing decisions and the aftermath.

"She decides priorities."

This quality, of course, has never been more critical. There are countless numbers of professionals and managers who work six days a week, fourteen hours a day and seem to get nothing done. Promote people who have a proven track record of consistent execution. Drucker felt that managers should have only two key priorities at a time, as he knew no one who could juggle more than that. He urged managers to do one thing at a time, and when they completed their two top priorities, to make a new list because by that time the old priorities were already outdated.

Four More Rituals of a Natural

Drucker had very definite ideas on what makes naturals tick. In addition to the three qualities he described to me during our interview (above), he had written extensively about the qualities he most closely associated with effective management. Here is a summary of his best advice (for a more complete analysis of Drucker's leadership ideal, see chapter 9):

1. **Naturals consistently ask themselves and their colleagues, "What do I need to do to maximize my contributions to the firm?"**
   Explained Drucker, "Effective executives find themselves asking other people in the organization, their superiors, their subordinates, but above all, their colleagues in other areas: 'What contribution from me do you require to make your contribution to the organization?'"

2. **Naturals know that the right question is more important than finding the right answer.**
   That's vintage Drucker. "For there are few things as useless—if not as dangerous—as the right answer to the wrong question. Nor is it enough to find the right answer. More important and more difficult is to make effective the course of action decided upon. Management is not concerned with knowledge for knowledge's sake; it is concerned with performance."

3. **Naturals understand that when the seas get rough, they do not hold another meeting.**

   Instead they take control by setting the right course and making sure that all hands are rowing in the right direction.

4. **Naturals know that morale and organizational culture is their responsibility.**

   Effective managers lead by example by making sure they do "*what* is right," and they care not at all about "*who* is right." These types of beliefs must be converted into values and communicated clearly throughout the firm.

When Naturals Run Out

Drucker spent much time thinking and talking about naturals, born leaders who needed no coaching to manage effectively. Prior to the 1870s, before the advent of the large corporation, there was not a need for large numbers of managers. But later, as the number of corporations multiplied, there was a much greater demand for managers. Drucker's earliest books helped to train high-profile managers for such companies as GE and Hewlett-Packard.

For a long time there were no middle managers. There was simply top management and a massive number of semi-skilled or unskilled workers beneath them. Pierre S. du Pont (1870–1954) created middle management in order to keep the company's best workers from leaving.

Drucker described his idea of a natural: a natural knows how to place people where they can make the greatest contributions. They are individuals who could hire and fire without getting upset, and they know how to set—and stick to—one or two priorities at a time. Naturals know how to ask the tough questions and make the difficult decisions, particularly when things go wrong. They know that the morale of the organization and the culture of the organization (or unit) is their responsibility.

Chapter 6

The Jeffersonian Ideal

> "In making and moving things . . . knowledge and service work, partnership with the responsible worker is the only way. . . ."

Drucker inserted dignity into the managerial equation from the beginning of his business book writing career and never wavered. Before him, workers were not seen as a resource or an asset. That was one of the key themes of his earliest works, and a major departure from the conventional wisdom of pre-1940s corporate America.

Jeffersonian democracy (derived, of course, from America's third president) argued for a representative democracy that favored the rights of the individual, or common man. Jefferson was "the man who defined America's meaning," asserted David N. Mayer, professor of law and history at Capital University. He added that "the Jeffersonian philosophy is clearly one of reason, individualism, liberty and limited government."

In Jefferson's first inaugural address in March 1801, he argued for uniting "in common efforts for the common good." He added "the minority possess their equal rights, which equal laws must protect, and to violate which would be oppression." He then urged his "fellow citizens to unite with one heart and one mind."

Much of Drucker's first business book, *Concept of the Corporation* (1946), is devoted to a Jeffersonian-like argument for the dignity of the individual over the cold "representative institution" of the era. Argued Drucker, "If the big-business corporation is America's representative social institution it must realize these basic beliefs of American society . . . it must give status and function to the individual, and it must give him the justice of equal opportunities. . . . Individual dignity and fulfillment in an industrial society can only be given in and through work."

Drucker also wrote of "equality" as a "specifically American phenomenon for which no parallel can be found in Europe. It explains those features of American society which have always struck visitors from abroad." Drucker then describes his perception of this phenomenon: a friendliness, an absence of envy, the absence of awe for the people at the top of the ladder. "Whatever its [equality's] origin, it pervades all American life. It shows in small details as the general accessibility of even the highest official and the absence of special elevators for the bosses in office buildings, and in such major traits as the deep resentment against anyone—man or nation—who throws his weight around."

These words are as pertinent today as they were when Drucker wrote them in 1946. Today top managers are more accessible and communicate more often with both managers and workers than ever before. And there is indeed a "deep resentment" for any "man or nation that throws his weight around." Most large organizations have gotten rid of the autocratic, arrogant snob who does nothing but bark orders and chastise underlings. The reasons are obvious: condescending managers accomplish much less than the CEO who works in collaboration and partnership with his or her management teams.

To be clear, Drucker never argued for a democratic workplace in which its participants get to vote on every key decision. He knew from his study of Alfred Sloan and GM that nothing was more important to a company's future than the quality and decision-making ability of its top management team (which is also a firm's costliest investment).

However, how a management team is organized and how it manages people are the critical factors, reasoned Drucker: "Any institution has to be organized so as to bring out talents and capacities within the organization; to encourage men to take the initiative, give them a chance to show what they can do, and a scope within which to grow; and finally, to offer them rewards in the form of advancement and of social and economic standing which put a definite premium on the willingness and ability to assume responsibility."

Many years later Drucker noted that "more and more of the input we need will not be from people or organizations that we control, but from people and organizations with which we have a relationship, a partnership—people whom we cannot command."

During our interview he spoke at length of his students and their careers. It was apparent that he had counseled hundreds of his students and followed their careers with great pride. The humanity he injected into his management books was not just management theory; it was how he taught, lived, and mentored. Drucker called himself the world's worst manager, but had he managed, say, a large corporation, he would have treated all employees with dignity. He also had one other indispensable quality of the first-rate manager: he had more humility than anyone I have ever met.

History Through Drucker's Eyes

In order to fully comprehend how Drucker wrote—and rewrote—the rules of management, it is important to understand the management models that were in place when he arrived on the scene in the 1940s.

During our interview Drucker delivered a quick but compelling course in management history. As was his penchant with his own books, he was quick to shine the spotlight on others who had come before him, the people whose philosophies and ideas set the stage for his own.

He heaped praise on one early management pioneer who had stressed the human aspects of work: "There was Mary

Parker Follett (1868–1933). She was totally forgotten—*totally*," he emphasized. "She had been suppressed. Not just forgotten. She was so contrary to the mentality of the thirties, which focused on conflict and adversarial relations that her emphasis on conflict resolution was simply unacceptable," declared Drucker.

Mary Parker Follett argued for "power with" instead of "power over" and coined such phrases as "authority and power" and "conflict resolution." She saw organizations as consisting of "group networks" rather than hierarchical autocracies. Perhaps that explains why Drucker called her a "prophet of management."

However, the most influential, yet controversial, management figure of the early twentieth century was Frederick Taylor (1856–1915), known as the Father of Scientific Management.

Taylor started with something he called time studies, which also became known as time and motion studies. These entailed studying workers performing tasks and timing each component of each task to the hundredth of a second. Taylor said that he could find the "one best way" to do any task. He started with workers shoveling sand. Before Taylor, shovels were designed in an unsystematic fashion. Their size and shape was arbitrary. Taylor determined that the ideal load per shovel of sand was 21.5 pounds, and he designed shovels to lift precisely that amount, thereby making workers more efficient.

Drucker summarized Taylor's main contribution as follows: "Taylor applied to manual operations the principles that machine designers during the nineteenth century had learned to apply to the work of a tool; he identified the work to be done; broke it down into its individual operations; designed the right way to do each operation; and finally he put the operations together, this time in the sequence in which they could be done fastest and most economically." In sum, concluded Drucker, "Taylor put knowledge to work to make the manual worker productive."

Taylor's *Principles of Scientific Management* was published in 1911 and influenced a great many practitioners, including Henry Ford. (Ford had called on Taylor to do time and motion studies at his automobile plant in order to streamline his assembly line, which turned out 15 million identical black Model Ts between 1908 and 1927.)

Another management thinker often associated with Taylor is France's Henri Fayol (1841–1925), who headed a coal mining company. Drucker credits the French management theorist with being the first to understand the need for structure in organizations. His fourteen principles of management (which included concepts such as "authority" and "unity of command") received a great deal of attention in Europe and the United States.

Taylor and scientific management had the most pervasive and enduring effect on how things would be manufactured in the twentieth century. Most of today's introductory management textbooks devote several pages to Taylor's scientific management and Henri Fayol's fourteen points, far more than is allotted to Drucker (as mentioned earlier, Drucker is lucky to get a few lines or a footnote in any textbook). This has been the case for decades, leaving one to wonder what the management textbooks of, say, a century hence will look like.

But in these management models, pointed out Drucker in the late 1950s, "Management was seen as a result rather than a cause, and as a response to needs rather than as a creator of opportunity."

The Limits of an Assembly-line Mentality

Despite Taylor's achievements, he would later be condemned for several of his ideas, particularly those that diminished the value and dignity of the individual. Taylor's creation valued fractions of seconds more than the ideas and values of the workers, whom he called helpers. There was "no such thing as skill in making and moving things," argued Taylor. Since all work was the same, and all workers were the same, any able individual could be taught to be a "first-rate man."

As a result of these unpopular ideas, Taylor would also be vilified by the academic elite (with the exception of latter-day management textbook authors). The notion that skill did not matter was simply *un-American*. It is hard to imagine a less popular belief in the United States, a country that values winning above almost all else. And criticism of Taylor was not limited to academia. As Drucker pointed out, even comedian Charlie

Chaplin poked fun at the foibles of the assembly line in the silent film *Modern Times*.

According to David Montgomery, the Farnam Professor of History at Yale University, "Taylor was not a charlatan, but his ideological message required the suppression of all evidence of worker's dissent . . . or of any human motives or aspirations other than those his vision of progress could encompass." That explains why Drucker viewed an assembly-line mentality as an enemy to everything he held dear, from original thought to the morale of the workforce.

Drucker changed the calculus—and the conversation. *Concept of the Corporation* made a forceful argument for the humanization of the workplace (Part II of that book is titled "The Corporation as Human Effort") and an equally strong argument against rote ways to get things done.

An assembly-line mentality "deprives a worker of satisfaction," Drucker asserted. He also argued that the most "efficient" assembly-line workers were more "machine-like" and "less human" than their coworkers. This sounds obvious now, but in an age when assembly lines were the best way to mass-produce anything, Drucker's views represented a significant departure from other management theorists.

It is unfortunate that a book that humanized the workplace was dismissed by the academic elite. According to *Economist* editors John Micklethwait and Adrian Wooldridge, *Concept of the Corporation* "further alienated turf-minded American academics:

economists regarded it as vulgar sociology, and political scientists dismissed it as economics gone mad." That explains why Drucker's career got sidetracked from the start.

The biggest takeaway from Drucker's early works is his everpresent awareness that organizations are social institutions made up not of the cogs, as in Frederick Taylor's assembly lines, but of people with needs and goals and strengths.

Drucker's contention that management was a "practice" and a "social discipline," and not a science, would change the course of the field of management.

He was also among the first to write of the importance of morale in an organization. In *The Practice of Management* (1954), he wrote: "We speak of 'leadership' and of the 'spirit' of a company, but leadership is given by managers ... and the spirit is made by the spirit within the management group."

Responsibility was always an important part of the managerial equation to Drucker: "It does not matter whether the worker wants responsibility or not. The enterprise must demand it of him. The enterprise needs performance; and now that it can no longer use fear, it can get it only by encouraging, by inducing, if need be by pushing, the worker into responsibility."

Don't Take "What to Do" for Granted

George Elton Mayo (1880–1949) was a psychologist and sociologist and professor of industrial research at Harvard University for more than two decades (1926–47). His work included the well-known Hawthorne Studies,* built on work done by theorist Mary Parker Follett. Both felt that omitting the human part of management was a serious flaw of the management models of the day. Mayo would later emerge as the father of what would be known as the Human Relations movement.

However, as Drucker pointed out, none of the human relation theorists went far enough: "When Frederick Taylor started what later became scientific management…it never occurred to him to ask 'What is the task? Why do it?' All he asked was 'How is it done?' Almost fifty years later, Harvard's George Elton Mayo (1880–1949) set out to demolish scientific management and replace it with what later came to be called human relations. But, like Taylor, he never asked 'What is the task? Why do it?' In making and moving things the task is always taken for granted."

Put another way, before Drucker, management was a one-dimensional discipline. The theorists were concerned with the best way to build things, not what to build or what not to build. Scientific management versus human relations boiled down to a debate on *how* best to do something, not *what* to do. But to Drucker, who regarded management as a practice and not a science, what to do was at least as important as how to do it.

This is vintage Drucker. One of his greatest gifts was his

---

* Conducted between 1927 and 1932, the Hawthorne Studies showed that workers who knew they were being studied performed at higher levels than those not under observation.

tendency to question every assumption and abandon those that were no longer relevant. Of course, strategy was the purview of management. When Alfred Sloan beat Henry Ford in the 1920s it was because of a superior segmentation strategy. (Drucker was no fan of Ford. He asserted that Ford mismanaged the company because he did not believe in managers.)

The Partnership Imperative

Prior to World War II, management never asked workers about the tasks they performed or how they could be done better. Frederick Taylor assumed that both managers and workers were "dumb oxen." George Elton Mayo had more respect for managers, but felt workers to be "immature" and "maladjusted." He felt that workers needed the expertise of psychologists to tell them what to do.

However, as Drucker pointed out, World War II changed the game. With no foremen or engineers or psychologists to tell workers what to do (they also had been drafted and were serving in World War II), Drucker and his colleagues had no choice but to speak to workers one-on-one. Drucker admitted that he was immensely surprised by what the workers told them. They were neither dumb nor maladjusted (as had been suggested by Mayo). Instead, workers had a very strong sense of what they were doing and how they could do things better. The key was engaging workers—"asking them was the way to get started on productivity and quality," Drucker explained.

And times were changing quickly: "For twenty-five years, from the end of World War II to the end of the 1960s, a management boom swept over the entire world.... Management ... became a worldwide concern," explained Drucker.

IBM was one of the first large companies to buy into the assumption that its workers knew how to do things better. *Think* was the watchword at Big Blue early on. That was affirmed by a large engraved sign that read THINK placed above the door at the IBM Schoolhouse in the mid-to-late 1930s. The other words that greeted IBMers who entered the school were OBSERVE, DISCUSS, LISTEN and READ, but a THINK sign was on full display in every IBM office, according to Thomas J. Watson.

Later, in the 1950s and 1960s, Japanese companies followed suit by having their managers develop closer relationships with their people.

One could get away without communicating with workers on an assembly line, when each task was predetermined. However, as work grew increasingly complex, as the percentage of knowledge workers/specialists began to dominate organizations, management needed to engage workers in a way that had not occurred to them before: "In knowledge and service work, partnership with the responsible worker is the only way; nothing else will work at all," Drucker wrote.

Later he wrote that in the information age, partnering with workers and developing close working relationships is more important than ever: "It will become more and more important for these people to get together and actually meet one another and work with one another on an organized, systematic, scheduled basis. Long distance information does not replace face-to-face relationships. It makes them actually more important. It makes it more important for people to know what to expect from one another. It makes it more important for people to have trust in each other. And this means both systematic information—and especially any information about any change, and organized face-to face relationships, that is, opportunities to get to know one another and to understand one another."

The best modern-day model of a large organization partnering with its workers is Jack Welch's GE. Since Welch started reading Peter Drucker in the late 1970s it is not surprising that several of his best moves can be traced back to the late management pioneer. For example, look how closely Welch's words echo Drucker's:

> "The [workers] knew a great deal about the work they were doing, its logic and rhythm," wrote Drucker.

> Welch later said: "Those [workers] who actually did the work ... had some striking ideas on how things could be done better."

Welch's confidence in the individual was one of the sparks that led to his signature Work-Out initiative. Welch began implementing Work-Out after learning that elitist GE managers were not listening to workers in the late 1980s. That's when an exasperated Welch institutionalized the engagement of the workforce by GE management.

In Work-Out, hierarchy is turned on its head as workers tell managers how to do things better in a multiday, town hall event. The idea behind Work-Out is that every person in the organization has good ideas, but they need a platform from which to articulate them. Explains Welch: "If you are controlling two people and just getting them to do what you say, I'd get rid of you and keep those two. If there are three people I want three ideas. If you're only giving orders I will get only your ideas. I'd rather select from the ideas of three people."

In his final years Drucker expanded on his theme of delegation and partnering with knowledge workers. In an interview with Elizabeth Haas Edersheim, author of *The Definitive Drucker*, he said once managers delegate something they must resist the urge of taking over a task for that employee, even if the subordinate messes it up. As long as people are not doing anything unethical or illegal, they should be left to their own devices, unless they ask for help. "The risk must be taken if people are allowed to define their own paths," he said.

He took the partnership theme to its extreme when he added: "If you are uncomfortable with the idea of vesting people with the power to fire their boss, then you are not ready for the task of leadership in the next century."

———

What else can you do to help you implement Drucker's partnership principle? Try doing the following:

- **Keep your people in the loop.**
  In a more democratic workplace, people have access to information. Everyone wants to know what is happening "upstairs"—and you are your direct reports' best link to the rest of the company. Nothing is worse than a department of lost souls who have no idea how the company or their part of it is doing.

- **Before assigning goals to your people,
  ask them to draft their own.**
  When people have input into their own goals, they are more likely to buy into them and strive to achieve them.

- **Meet with your team regularly to explain how their
  work fits into the organization as a whole.**
  All employees want to know where their efforts fit into the bigger scheme of things. Biweekly meetings—over a brown bag lunch or delivered pizza—can give you a chance to tell your team how their efforts are contributing to the overall health of the company.

● **Engage your direct reports in frequent informal dialogue and provide candid feedback.**

Let your people know how they are doing. Take them out for a cup of coffee and start by telling them what they are doing best. By discussing how they are doing compared with their goals, you will be giving the type of feedback workers crave. (In chapter 8 we will get into the concept of managing around weaknesses.)

The Jeffersonian Ideal

Drucker's view of the corporation, and its relation to the employee and society, changed the calculus. Workers were not simply costs or cogs in a machine: "Everybody from the boss to the sweeper must be seen as equally necessary to the success of the common enterprise. At the same time the large corporation must offer equal opportunities for advancement." But even now, sixty years after Drucker wrote of these ideals, a certain percentage of employees and managers feel more like costs or cogs than resources and individuals.

Drucker made clear that knowledge workers had to focus on the key tasks that would help the organization succeed, and "eliminate everything else." In other words, the most effective people know what needs to be done and abandon everything else. Their managers can help them by asking them the following: "What is your greatest priority? What should it be? What should you be expected to contribute? What hampers you in doing your task and should be eliminated?" The last question is vital. In today's frenzied workplace, with blizzards of e-mails and meetings and ringing phones, knowing what one should *not* do is half the battle. Naturals do these things intuitively; however, the best managers should have these kinds of discussions with their people all the time. Sometimes helping one of your direct reports cut through red tape or removing a meaningless task can free him or her to pursue an important opportunity for the company.

Chapter 7

Abandon All but Tomorrow

"A critical question for leaders is, 'When do you stop pouring resources into things that have achieved their purpose?' The most dangerous traps for a leader are those near-successes where everybody says that if you just give it another big push it will go over the top."

This chapter showcases what I regard as one of Drucker's signature strategies. It will also illustrate how Drucker lived what he taught. He told me that after he wrote a book he never read it again. He abandoned it. When he had a new idea, he simply wrote a new book. The same was true in the choices he made in his life. His career was about abandoning the past in favor of the future. He turned down prestigious chairs at both Harvard and Stanford and never looked back.

He never reveled in past glory. There was no evidence of his past achievements on walls or the halls of his home, at least not where visitors could see it. It was all about tackling new challenges.

Drucker told me he lamented only one thing: a book he didn't write. "The best book I have not written was a book called *Managing Ignorance*. It would have been a wonderful book but a very difficult book." He told me he began to write it but never finished it. This book would have been a departure for Drucker, since it would highlight all the missteps that managers make, forcing him to focus on weaknesses rather than strengths. Perhaps that's the reason he never finished it.

Abandonment Is Not Sexy

Ask most Drucker fans to list Drucker's three most important ideas and they are unlikely to mention his concept of purposeful abandonment. Abandonment is not as catchy as Drucker's Law ("there is only one valid definition of business purpose: to create a customer") or management by objectives, the Drucker concept that gained great popularity in the decades following World War II.

Nor is abandonment the sort of concept that sounds impressive in a senior manager's presentation. Few managers brag about a product or idea that they abandoned, yet abandonment decisions have cleared the way for some of the most successful products in history.

However, because of what Drucker calls investment in managerial ego, managers resist abandonment. That's because abandonment runs counter to what managers have been taught all of their careers: to grow revenues at all cost. Growth, both top line and bottom line, is the lifeblood of a company. Abandoning any product line appears to shrink sales and profits. However, that is an incorrect perception, particularly in the long run.

Drucker insists that too many managers hold on to yesterday for too long, and their businesses suffer as a result. Firms stick with their cash cows until they are made irrelevant by competitors. Those that cannot abandon yesterday are doomed to irrelevance, contends Drucker.

The First Step in a Growth Policy

As Drucker asserts, "The first step in a growth policy is not to decide where and how to grow. *It is to decide what to abandon.* In order to grow, a business must have a systematic policy to get rid of the outgrown, the obsolete, [and] the unproductive."

Not abandoning ideas and/or products whose time has passed has led to some of the costliest blunders ever. For example, in the early 2000s both Ford and GM aggressively pursued their strategy of producing record numbers of gas-guzzling SUVs, despite a growing green movement and soaring gas prices. Toyota, alternatively, focused on developing new hybrid technology and found ways to make hybrid cars like the Prius affordable for the masses. Toyota's leaders knew that hybrids were the key to decreasing carbon emissions and reducing fuel consumption, and they were willing to accept smaller profit margins to become the leading player in this burgeoning market.

Prius, the first Toyota hybrid, launched in Japan in 1997 and was rolled out worldwide in 2001. The new car was a hit from the start. It garnered several awards, including Car of the Year Japan in 1997–98, North American Car of the Year in 2004, and European Car of the Year in 2005.

The results were dramatic—even unthinkable only a decade earlier. Prius played a role in catapulting Toyota to the world's number one automaker (a position GM had held for seventy years), while Ford and GM continued to falter and rack up record losses. (Ford lost $12.7 billion in 2006, and GM lost $38.7 billion in 2007. Toyota earned $13.1 billion in the first nine months of 2007 alone.)

In December of 2006, Ford CEO Alan Mulally traveled to Japan to meet with Toyota chairman Fujio Cho. Mulally said that he had sought the Toyota chairman's advice on how to streamline Ford's manufacturing operations. However, the company's problems went deeper than manufacturing.

Detroit's inability to abandon the cash cows that had outlived their usefulness cost them dearly. According to Drucker, "One should . . . abandon yesterday's breadwinner before one really wants to, let alone before one has to." Detroit certainly did not heed Drucker's advice, despite the fact that it was first offered in 1964.

By not aggressively pursuing hybrids earlier, U.S. carmakers missed a golden opportunity. Hindsight is 20/20, but had GM, Ford, and Chrysler shifted some resources from larger SUVs to fuel-stingy hybrids, they would not have dug themselves such a deep hole. Certainly, there were signs that the automobile market was undergoing fundamental changes. Talk of alternatives to traditional fossil fuels has been around since the 1970s and heated up again in the 1990s.

The most effective managers learn to read the tea leaves and prepare their organizations to exploit new opportunities created by new realities.

Explains Drucker: "Maximizing opportunities shows how to move the business from yesterday to today—thereby making it ready for the new challenges of tomorrow. It shows the existing activities that should be pushed and those that should be abandoned. And it brings out the new things that might multiply results in the market or in the company's field of knowledge."

Rewrite Last Month's Manual

One of the secrets behind Toyota's great success is its deep-rooted tradition for finding a better way to do things—an ingrained culture in which all are taught to abandon yesterday's methods in search of a new way of doing things.

Toyota's founder, Sakichi Toyoda, was a self-taught inventor who started the company not with cars but by making a better loom for women to use in weaving. He was what Drucker called a natural, as he constantly searched for better ways to do things (he got his first loom patent in 1890). Ultimately he would acquire more than one hundred patents and become a world-class inventor in the same league as Thomas Edison and Henry Ford.

The five founding precepts of the company, created in 1935, still guide Toyota today. One holds that workers "should be ahead of the times, through endless creativity, inquisitiveness, and pursuit of improvement."

Improvement and abandonment are two sides of the coin. To improve, one must abandon what works less well and do what works better.

Taiichi Ohno, a former executive vice president and key player behind Toyota's signature manufacturing system, said, "Something is wrong if workers do not look around each day, find things that are tedious or boring, and then rewrite the procedures. Even last month's manual should be out of date."

Other managers recognized that Toyota's patented manufacturing method, the Toyota Production System, known also as TPS, was worthy of study. Companies as diverse as John Deere and Wal-Mart have analyzed and studied TPS, and put aspects of it to work in their own organizations.

Inherent in TPS is the firm's long-standing commitment to *kaizen,* or continuous improvement. The key to continuous improvement is to develop people who constantly search for ways to rid the company of *munda,* or waste. Of course, all companies want to improve their products and processes. However, according to the book *How Toyota Became #1* by David Magee, "There is a distinct difference between approaching TPS as a mere manufacturing tool and using it as a guiding principle by which to live and work."

Kaizen is evident in all Toyota plants, where any worker is empowered to "stop the train" at the first sign of a problem. Toyota workers are urged to pull a cord that stops the assembly line in the face of a quality or safety issue. In the Toyota system, workers are not chastised for stopping the line; in fact, the opposite is true. They risk making a mistake by *not* stopping the line when they should. That's why the cord is pulled as many as five thousand times a day in any one Toyota plant on any given day.

At Toyota, the philosophy of improvement and abandoning what does not work is not restricted to the plant floor. That's where most companies go wrong. Firms that do not apply those same principles of kaizen to other aspects of their business often fail. At Toyota, one can see its signature manufacturing methods in almost every aspect of the firm's business.

According to Jim Press, the former president of Toyota Motor North America (and now president of Chrysler), "The factory is the most visible and the easiest place to identify [TPS] at work ... but the elements and the essence behind those principles are everywhere ... from the service department at a Lexus dealership to the security man on premises at Toyota Motor Sales USA in Torrance, California."

One other important part of the Toyota culture is called the

5 Whys. The 5 Whys is a method used in manufacturing to help find the root cause of a problem. The assumption is that asking only a few questions does not allow the manager to get to the source of a problem.

This method gained popularity in the 1970s, when other companies started to study and emulate Toyota's methods. Later the idea behind the 5 Whys evolved into more sophisticated quality methods, such as the statistically based Six Sigma program (the quality initiative pioneered by Motorola and popularized by GE). The 5 Whys is another tool that Toyota used to abandon the old and find better ways of getting things done.

In 2007, Toyota was the number three company on *Fortune's* list of most admired companies in the United States and number two overall worldwide (it had climbed six slots from the previous year). No doubt the company's tendency of embracing tomorrow and leaving yesterday behind has played a key role in its success.

Abandonment and Reality

Some managers are able to let go of the past better than others. Those that have the greatest difficulty abandoning things are often those unable to face reality. Dr. Sydney Finkelstein, author of *Why Smart Executives Fail*, conducted a six-year study and identified the two top causes of management failure. Both were directly related to the inability to face reality.

According to the study, organizations make their greatest missteps when the senior managers' mind-set throws off the firm's perception of reality. The second most common contributor to executive failure involves "delusional attitudes that keep this inaccurate reality in place."

Perhaps that explains why "face reality" was Jack Welch's first rule of business. At GE he repeated that mantra time and again, and it helped him to make the tough decisions that garnered him such accolades as Manager of the Century by *Fortune* magazine.

Welch's first decade as CEO of GE is a textbook case of purposeful abandonment. He sold off 117 businesses that did not fit his new vision of the company. For example, in 1984, he sold off GE Housewares, the division that was best known to American households (it made products like toasters and hair dryers). When asked how he could sell off a piece of America to foreigners, he answered unequivocally: *"In the year 2000, would you rather be in toasters or CT scanners?"*

That question was derived from a classic Drucker litmus test:

If we did not do this already, would we go into it now, knowing what we know?

And if the answer is no, the organization has to ask: And what do we do now? It has to do something, not just make another study.

These appeared in Drucker's *Post-Capitalist Society*, and were variations on similar questions Drucker had asked about entering new markets. Drucker felt strongly that there was only one way for an organization to be disciplined enough to deal with these key questions, which he elaborated on in the early to mid-1990s: "Every organization of today has to build into its very structure *the management of change*. It has to build in organized abandonment of everything it does. . . . Increasingly, organizations will have to *plan* abandonment rather than try to prolong a life of a successful policy, practice, or product—something which so far only a few Japanese companies have faced up to."

That Drucker imperative becomes a powerful business tool when used by managers who are serious about abandonment. If answered honestly, it will light the way by showing managers which businesses or markets to exit. The keys are to make sure that management faces reality and that the company has a specific strategic plan that keeps it focused on what it does best. Explains Drucker: "A strategy enables an institution to be purposefully opportunistic. If what looks like an opportunity does not advance the strategic goal of the institution, it is not an opportunity. It is a distraction."

How else can you be sure that you are staying ahead of the curve by abandoning the obsolete? Consider the following:

● **Abandon nonperformers and/or those who do not live up to the company values.**

Not only products and processes can be abandoned. Jim Collins, author of *Good to Great*, explained that a manager's top priority is getting the right people on the bus and the wrong people off. Decades earlier, Drucker had advocated firing anyone, especially any manager, who fails to set the right example: "To let [such] a man stay on corrupts the others. It is grossly unfair to the whole organization," wrote Drucker.

● **Abandon "milk cows" when they begin to deteriorate.**

Drucker urged managers to put the greatest amount of a firm's resources behind "high opportunity" products/ product lines that can "pay for their costs many times over" (he also called these "push priorities"). He explained that "also-rans...have to make do with what they have—or with less. They are put on 'milking status'; as long as they yield results, they will be kept—and milked. They will, however, not be 'fed.' And as soon as these 'milk cows' go into rapid decline, they should be slaughtered."

● **Train direct reports to practice purposeful abandonment.**

You can't do it alone. You will need to enlist those closest to the market—and the customer—to constantly search out and identify those products or product lines that are fading; at the same time, they should also be asked to contribute ideas that can lead to tomorrow's opportunities and innovations.

Abandon All but Tomorrow

Abandonment is one of the keys to understanding Drucker because it is such a fundamental part of who he was. Purposeful abandonment brings together a number of key Drucker principles. For example, abandonment involves the discipline of consistently asking the right questions: "When you think you have all the answers, you don't even ask the questions," said Drucker. He never stopped asking the right questions, and urged managers to question every assumption, starting with the most basic. For example, Drucker wrote, "Nothing may seem simpler or more obvious than to answer what a company's business is. . . . Actually 'what is our business' is almost always a difficult question which can be answered only after hard thinking and studying. And the right answer is usually anything but obvious." Defining your business involves making tough decisions about which markets to exit and which to enter; which areas to "push" and which to abandon. Last, no organization can truly abandon yesterday unless it has given "somebody in senior management the specific assignment to work on tomorrow as an entrepreneur and innovator."

Chapter 8

Auditing Strengths

"In knowledge work, above all, one therefore has to staff from strength. And this means constant attention to placing knowledge workers where what they can do will produce results and make a contribution."

In the latter half of the 1990s and early 2000s, thousands upon thousands of pages were written by noteworthy authors extolling the virtues of building both leaders and organizations by focusing on strengths.

However, decades earlier, long before anyone else thought to write about it, Drucker had made it clear that it was the duty of all responsible managers to focus on strengths: "Nothing destroys the spirit of an organization faster than focusing on people's weaknesses rather than on their strengths, building on disabilities rather than on abilities. *The focus must be on strength... the greatest mistake is to try to build on weakness,*" Drucker asserted.

That sounds logical, even intuitive. However, the majority of today's managers spend most of their time trying to fix weaknesses rather than build on strengths. In fact, most large organizations not only encourage this behavior, they institutionalize it by incorporating it into many of the company's informal and formal reviews and processes. As a result, managers are trained to focus on employees' flaws rather than enhance their strengths.

This chapter will explore Drucker's early work on strengths theory, and how it shaped other aspects of his writings, such as leadership selection and development. It will also showcase effective modern-day leaders, such as Procter & Gamble's A. G. Lafley, and how they have used this part of the Drucker playbook to strengthen their own organizations.

The Strengths Revolution

In the last few years one author team has won fortune and acclaim by starting what they called a strengths revolution. Marcus Buckingham and Donald Clifton, authors of *Now, Discover Your Strengths*, start their best-selling book with the following declaration: "We wrote this book to start a revolution, a strengths revolution. At the heart of this revolution is a simple decree: the great organization must not only accommodate the fact that each employee is different, *it must capitalize on these differences.* It must watch for clues to each employee's natural talents and then position and develop each employee so that his or her talents are transformed into bona fide strengths."

Almost five decades earlier, Drucker wrote: "One can only build on strength. One can achieve only by doing. Appraisal must therefore aim first and foremost on bringing out what a man can do … a man should never be appointed to a managerial position if his vision focuses on people's weaknesses rather than on their strengths." Later he added: "We will have to learn to build organizations in such a manner that any man who has strength in one important area is capable of putting it to work."

As we have seen with so many ideas, Drucker got there first. This does not mean that the contributions of Buckingham and Clifton are not genuine, or that they did not add significantly to the body of knowledge. It simply means that they built their strengths revolution on an idea whose provenance can be traced to Drucker.

To the credit of Buckingham and Clifton, they acknowledged Drucker's contribution by including the following quote from him (Drucker) on the front inside flap of their book: "Most Americans do not know what their strengths are. They look at you with a blank stare, or they respond in terms of subject knowledge, which is the wrong answer."

Audit Your Own Strengths

In my meeting with Drucker, it was abundantly clear that the strengths doctrine he espoused five decades earlier was still very much a part of his belief system. He knew himself, his strengths, and spent a good part of the day explaining how he had built on his own strengths in his lifelong journey to create a new discipline (although he was quick to admit that he did not set out to do anything that grandiose).

He knew that his greatest contribution—his greatest strength—was to create the discipline of management before anyone else had pulled it together. "So what I really did . . . in systematic form, [was recognize] management as a new social institution."

Knowing one's strengths comes with one additional advantage: knowing what one does *not* want to do. For example, few aspiring professors or scholars would turn down Harvard, but Drucker did because he knew himself and his strengths. Drucker knew that cases were a big part of the course work at Harvard, and he told me how much he hated cases. The other reason Drucker cited for snubbing Harvard was that it did not allow professors to consult back then, and Drucker was not about to give up what he loved doing.

Leaders who focus on strength not only know what to do, argued Drucker, they also know what they should avoid. "Waste as little effort as possible on improving areas of low competence," urged Drucker. "It takes far more energy and far more work to improve from incompetence to low mediocrity than it takes to improve from first-rate performance to excellence. . . . The energy and resources—and time—should instead go into making a competent person into a star performer."

Drucker's assertion—that it is easier to turn competent managers into star performers than turn incompetent managers into competent ones—was confirmed by two other authors, Jack Zenger and Joseph Folkman, in their 2002 book, *The Extraordinary Leader*. In researching their book, the duo compiled two hundred thousand 360-degree evaluations that were completed on twenty thousand individuals. They contrasted the top 10 percent with the bottom 10 percent and found that managers who had no real perceived strength were rated in the bottom third of all managers in their organization.

However, if a manager was perceived to have even one strength (or competence), that manager's rating went from the 34th percentile all the way up to the 68th percentile. If the leader had three strengths, his or her rating soared to the 84th percentile. Explains Jack Zenger: "The really powerful message here is to be a highly effective leader inside of an organization; you need to be perceived as exceptional at 3 or 4 things, not 34 things." That conclusion, backed up by boatloads of data, proves what Drucker posited decades earlier, starting in the 1950s.

Rethink Performance Reviews

Few managers or employees look forward to annual review time. In fact, most dread it. Managers hate the process because of the mounds of paperwork, and the common tendency is to wait until the last possible minute to complete them (when HR

Seven Tips for Building on Strength

One of Drucker's prescient business tenets is: *"All development is self-development."* This means that it is every individual's responsibility to do whatever is necessary to gain the mind-set, training, and initiative to grow professionally. The key is to do that by focusing on strengths. Here are seven ideas on how to do that, excerpted directly from Drucker's writings:

1. List your major contributions over the last two to three years.
2. Make a list of the four to six specific tasks and responsibilities that you are most accountable for at your company.
3. Ask for the most demanding assignments.
4. Examine the best in yourself before searching out the best in others.
5. Do not fear strong colleagues or ambitious subordinates.
6. Don't resent talent—surround yourself with the best.
7. Become a genuine doer and do not waste energy putting others down.

and senior management start screaming for them). People hate performance reviews because no one enjoys criticizing others (or being criticized), which is what most performance reviews are all about. These issues have conspired to make annual review time a highly uncomfortable ritual, rather than the genuine opportunity it affords managers who are willing to change their mind-set surrounding this very important exercise.

There is some irony that Drucker, the inventor of the most widely used appraisal system of the twentieth century, management by objectives, or MBOs, felt strongly from the outset that a manager who focuses only on weaknesses is a "mismanager." Simply pinpointing problematic traits or identifying things that people do poorly is no way to enhance performance. "One cannot do anything with what one cannot do. One cannot achieve anything with what one does not do.... Appraisal must therefore aim first and foremost on bringing out what a man can do," wrote Drucker early on.

There are some companies that truly live by Drucker's strengths doctrine. At the University of Toyota in Torrance, California, strengths training has been a prominent part of the curriculum for a decade. In 1999, the company offered a pilot program focused on identifying people's strengths, and the response was off the charts. Word of the program spread like wildfire and within weeks there was a year-long waiting list, reported Mike Morrison, the dean of the University of Toyota. Today managing on strengths is ingrained into the DNA of Toyota's leaders.

The most prominent example of how the University of Toyota lives by Drucker's strengths doctrine is found in the performance review process. At the University of Toyota, managers are trained to manage around people's weak spots. They are trained to focus instead on people's strengths and find ways to de-emphasize their weaknesses. This represents a sea change in performance reviews, and Morrison says that this is still a work in progress. However, there is no doubt that the University of Toyota is on the right track and miles ahead of most organizations.

Your Back Room Is Somebody's Front Room

Drucker had an uncanny knack for sizing up other people's strengths. As will be discussed at length in chapter 10, he spoke extensively about GE and Jack Welch the day we talked, including detailing Welch's greatest personal qualities: "He has that great ability to keep quiet." Drucker sat in meetings with Welch and told me that he (Welch) would sit for hours and not utter a single word, except to ask for clarification for a point or to summarize the main points. However, he would make sure the meeting ended with clear assignments. Drucker said that was vital, something he learned from Alfred Sloan. Since most meetings "end in murkiness," it is essential that leaders make sure people leave meetings with very clear action plans.

Drucker also knew Welch's strengths transcended the more immediate—as CEO he maintained his strategic perspective. He had that rare ability to recognize an organization in dire need of an overhaul, even when everyone else felt the status quo was just fine.

When Welch became CEO in 1981, Drucker's lessons were fresh in his mind. Perhaps that explains why he grasped what had eluded others: despite the fact that management textbooks heralded GE as the model organization, he knew the company had to be "blown up" (as he later called it) or reinvented.

What few people (including myself) knew was that just weeks prior to assuming the top job, Welch had visited with Drucker at the latter's home in Claremont, California. Drucker described to me that visit in some detail. It was during that meeting that Drucker advised Welch to go on offense (see chapter 10 for more on this subject). However, even going on offense requires abandonment. Remember the Druckerism, "The first step in any growth policy is identifying what to abandon."

Years later, in the late 1990s, Welch learned another critical lesson from Drucker: stick to what you do best and let others do the rest. Welch put this under the heading "Your Back Room Is Somebody Else's Front Room" in his memoir. Welch credited Drucker with the idea and added that it was something they practiced at GE. Rather than own a cafeteria, outsource it to a food company. If printing is not your strength, let a print shop handle it. The key is to know your organization's strengths—where it can add real value—and make sure to deploy your best people and the company's resources in those areas.

Drucker biographer Elizabeth Haas Edersheim put it more

simply. She explained that Welch had told her, "Peter had made him conscious of GE's ability to work with another organization that was excited about something that GE found boring."

That explains why Welch hired a firm in India to do GE's programming twenty years before India became the go-to place for outsourcing. Once Welch realized that his company was never going to be the best at programming, he found a company that excelled at it. He clearly understood Drucker's strengths doctrine when he commented: "Back rooms by definition will never be able to attract *your best*. We converted ours into someone else's front room and insisted on getting *their best*."

Over the years, Welch abandoned the insularity that had defined GE in the decades leading up to his appointment. He insisted that managers look outside for answers to the company's thorniest challenges. "Someone, somewhere, has to have a better answer" became a common Welch refrain. That explains part of Welch's extraordinary success: auditing the company's strengths became a reflex, something that got embedded deep into the fabric of the company's culture.

That's a lesson that big box retailer Home Depot took to heart. Knowing that logistics and shipping are not among the company's strengths, its management hired UPS to handle everything that has to do with shipping. That has allowed both companies to stick to their knitting, with Home Depot customers being the main beneficiaries of this decision.

One more example of a leader who builds on strength is James McNerney. The current CEO of Boeing, McNerney was a great leader at GE who worked with Jack Welch for years, but didn't get the nod to succeed him. However, he went on to head 3M and Boeing and did good things for both companies (even though he was at 3M for a relatively short stint of four years). How does he maximize people's contributions? By giving—and following—this advice: "Expect a lot, inspire people, ask them to take the values that are important to them at home or at church and bring them to work."

Take a Strengths Audit

What kind of a leader are you—someone who builds on the strengths of your people and organization? Or someone who spends too much time consumed by the negatives? Take the following unscientific strengths audit to get the answer (5 means strongly agree, 1 designates strongly disagree):

1. I feel that I know my own strengths and look for ways to leverage those strengths to achieve organizational goals.

2. I seek out ways to enhance my strengths, either by practice, through a mentor, or by classroom training.

3. In the part of the organization I am responsible for (team, division, or unit), I have my best people working on the areas that offer the firm the greatest upside opportunities.

4. Taking a page from Jack Welch, I outsource to others those tasks and activities that belong in someone else's front room rather than my back room.

5. When engaging in informal one-on-one discussions with my direct reports, I am more likely to discuss the things they do best, rather than focus on their weaker points.

6. In departmental meetings that I host, I focus on the positive aspects of the team's performance and accomplishments.

7. I encourage my direct reports to seek out training in areas in which they already excel. I allocate a percentage of my annual department budget for training my direct reports and foster an atmosphere in which B-plus players can become A players.

Now add up your scores. In this very quick, anything-but-scientific audit, understand that your score is only an indicator of direction. But I will include some benchmarks to judge your results:

If you scored 28 or above, consider yourself a leader who leads on strengths.

If you scored 22–27, you take the issue of strengths seriously, but can get even better by working on those areas in which you scored yourself a 3 or lower.

If you scored 17–21, there is real room for improvement. Read over the seven statements again and write down some specific ideas on how you can improve.

If you scored below 17, you are a pessimist who spends your time dealing with petty issues and focusing on people's weaknesses. Read each of the seven statements above and write down three ways in which you can alter your mind-set and approach.

Auditing Strengths

Remember that there are many aspects of building on strengths. They involve understanding your own strengths and taking steps to make them stronger. (Remember the Druckerism "All development is self-development.") It means helping your direct reports to enhance their own strengths while managing around weaknesses. Building on strength also means being strategic in your staff assignments—putting your best people on projects that can yield the greatest results. Drucker warns that nonprofits, for example, put their best people "where there are no results." That unforced error is a common one and more prevalent in organizations in which change comes slowly. Conducting a simple strengths audit, say, biannually, can help managers make important adjustments at critical times (for example, when competing for a key client or creating a new product). Last, the strongest managers hire and promote the strongest people. Drucker reminds us of that when he writes that business titan Andrew Carnegie wanted to inscribe the following on his tombstone: "Here lies a man who knew how to put into his service more able men than he was himself."

Chapter 9

The Critical Factor?

"Leaders don't start out asking, 'What do I want to do?' They ask, 'What needs to be done?' Then they ask, 'Of those things that would make a difference, which are right for me?' They don't tackle things they aren't good at. They make sure other necessities get done, but not by them."

Drucker's stance on the topic of leadership and charisma had not changed in half a century. He contended that people put too much emphasis on charisma and too little in the things that really matter (for example, character, an ability to get things done). "Leadership is not magnetic personality ... it is not 'making friends and influencing people'—that is salesmanship," asserted Drucker. Leadership is the lifting of a man's vision to higher sights, the raising of a man's performance to a higher standard, the building of man's personality beyond its normal limitations."

Drucker also argued that there was no such thing as "leadership quality or leadership personality." What he meant was that everyone was different, and there was not one set of rigid characteristics that defined all leaders. He felt Harry Truman did not have an ounce of charisma ("as bland as a dead mackerel" was how he described the thirty-third president), but he was "absolutely trustworthy" and was "worshipped."

Drucker also felt that Franklin D. Roosevelt, Winston Churchill, George Marshall, Dwight Eisenhower, Bernard Montgomery, and Douglas MacArthur were exceptional leaders during the Second World War. However, "no two of them shared any 'personality traits' or any 'qualities.' "

The most charismatic leaders of the twentieth century, wrote Drucker, were Hitler, Stalin, Mao, and Mussolini. He called them "misleaders." In addition to Truman, he felt that Ronald Reagan was one of the most effective presidents of the last century. "His great strength was not charisma, as is commonly thought," Drucker explained, "but that he knew exactly what he could do and what he could not do."

The Key Is Effectiveness

In a 2004 interview with Forbes.com, Drucker said he was the first modern-day management writer to talk about leadership— fifty years earlier. Since then he argued that there was too much focus on leadership and "not enough on effectiveness." He was right. Type in the word *leadership* on an Amazon.com book search and you get close to a *quarter million* hits. As a book category, leadership books are perennial strong sellers, which explains why publishers are so enamored with the topic and why there is such a glut of them on the market.

How did Drucker define leadership? "A leader is somebody who has followers." That was how he defined leadership in several of his books. According to James O'Toole, who served as managing director of the Booz Allen Hamilton Strategic Leadership Center, "There is something profound in this insight . . . would-be leaders can focus their efforts on learning what they must *do* to attract followers. There is no more practical starting point."

Drucker later put more meat on the bones when he added, "The foundation of effective leadership is thinking through the organization's mission, defining it, and establishing it, clearly and visibly." (Interestingly enough, Jack Welch's definition of leadership sounds a lot like Drucker's: Welch's leader is someone "who can articulate a vision and get others to carry it out." See the next chapter for more on Welch.)

Drucker summed up the difference between management and leadership in fewer than a dozen words, and repeated this riff throughout his career: "Management is doing things right; leadership is doing the right things."

Last, naturals (as we showed in chapter 5), and all truly effective leaders, are far more interested in "*what* is right than *who* is right . . . to put personality above the requirements of the work is corruption and corrupts," wrote Drucker.

He learned that lesson from GM's Alfred Sloan. Remember that Sloan was not the one who brought Drucker in to analyze his company in 1943 (the study that led to *Concept of the Corporation*). Sloan was in fact against it. However, once Drucker got there, Sloan told the promising young writer: "You tell us what you think is right. Don't worry about *who* is right. Don't worry whether this or that member of our management will like your recommendations or conclusions."

Drucker's Leadership Ideal

Drucker was consistently ahead of his time. In his first business book he wrote, "No institution can possibly survive if it needs geniuses or supermen to manage it.* It must be organized in such a way as to be able to get along under a leadership composed of average human beings. No institution can endure if it is under one-man rule."

He wrote that statement in 1946, in a book that made a convincing case for decentralization—and against purely hierarchical, autocratic organizations. He felt autocracy contributed to Henry Ford's demise. His firm ultimately got whipped by GM, failing because he attempted to run a large multibillion-dollar business without believing in managers.

---

* Interestingly enough, Drucker revisited the issue more than half a century later when he called GE's Jack Welch and Intel's Andy Grove "CEO supermen" in *Managing in the Next Society* (St. Martin's Press, 2002).

He also explained why leadership is more of an issue for corporations than other institutions: "In the modern corporation, the problem of leadership is not only more important than in other institutions, it is far more difficult. For the modern industrial enterprise needs many more leaders than institutions, and of high quality. At the same time, it does not automatically produce leaders either in sufficient numbers or of sufficient quality and experience."

He later added, "Leadership cannot be created or promoted. It cannot be taught or learned . . . management cannot create leaders. It can only create the conditions under which potential leadership qualities become effective; or it can stifle potential leadership."

Put another way, *great* leaders are born, not made. Drucker felt that naturals are scarce. He made those arguments in his first two business books, published in 1946 and 1954, respectively. However, his views on the topic would soften over the years. Greatness cannot be learned, but management could be taught. After all, he wrote all those books to help turn ordinary people into practicing managers. Remember that when he started out, he had searched libraries for books on management, but he found nothing, which is why he had to "make it up."

As discussed in chapter 5, Drucker understood that there were a limited number of naturals to run large companies. Drucker's work was instrumental in helping to create the managers that were desperately needed when the naturals ran out.

However, to be an effective leader, one needs to have the

stuff that leaders are made of, something that Drucker talked and wrote about for most of his life. As Drucker stated earlier, "Leadership is doing the right things." The most effective leaders, those who garnered Drucker's highest marks, had the following traits and tendencies:

Character First, Then Courage:

Anyone who knew or met Drucker knew that he was someone who lived by his own words. He walked the talk. He might have known nothing about "management from the inside" (his oft-repeated phrase), but that does not mean that he did not possess the qualities which he deemed indispensable for effective leadership.

The most basic of those qualities is character. Drucker had character in spades. According to *Good to Great* author Jim Collins, Drucker was "infused with this humanity, and above all ... a very, very deep compassion for the individual." That's about as good a definition for character as I can imagine.

Explains Drucker: "It is character through which leadership is exercised, it is character that sets the example." Drucker recognized early on that character is not something one can learn or acquire, as a leader cannot recover from a breach of integrity. "It is vision and moral responsibility that, in the last analysis, define the manager," he said.

Drucker felt that a leader also needed courage to make the tough decisions. It takes courage to abandon yesterday, to give up on things in which you have a vested interest, to change course midstream. According to Drucker biographer Elizabeth Haas Edersheim, Drucker liked to say that Jack Welch had the "courage of a lion" because of the drastic steps he took in transforming GE (selling off hundreds of businesses and eliminating well over a hundred thousand jobs).

Creates a Clear Mission:

The most effective leaders paint a clear picture of what needs to be done: "The foundation of effective leadership is thinking through the organization's mission, defining it, and establishing it, clearly and visibly," explained Drucker. "The leader sets the goals, sets the priorities, and sets and maintains the standards. He makes compromises, of course; indeed, effective leaders are pitifully aware that they are not in control of the universe (only misleaders—the Stalins, Hitlers, and Maos—suffer from that delusion). But before accepting a compromise, the effective leader has thought through what is right and what is desirable. The leader's first task is to be the trumpet that sounds a clear sound."

Instills Loyalty:

Drucker asserted that the most effective managers inspire loyalty throughout the ranks. Loyalty, however, cannot be bought. One must be worthy of it. To be so, managers must set high standards and live by example. There can be no breach of the values of the organization. Those managers who live the values of the organization can motivate their people to place the needs of the organization ahead of their own personal goals. Those leaders who inspire loyalty raise the morale of their people, which in turn enhances performance.

Remember that loyalty is a two-way street. Managers must practice what they preach by being loyal to their employees. This entails giving positive feedback, and monetary rewards and promotions when they are earned. In today's world, where there is a scarcity of talent, management must treat their best people as if they have multiple offers from competing firms, which is nearer to reality than most imagine.

Instilling fear is no way to manage anything. Those managers who lead by intimidation are part of yesterday, not today or tomorrow. That's because those people who fear for their jobs are unlikely to contribute meaningfully by trying new things.

Focuses on Strengths:

As discussed in the previous chapter, leaders focus on strengths: their own strengths, strengths of other people, and the strengths of the organization. Drucker said that one of the keys to effective management is to make an individual's "strength effective and their weaknesses irrelevant."

As an example, Drucker cited two U.S. presidents: "In picking their cabinets, both Franklin Roosevelt and Harry Truman said, in effect, never mind personal weaknesses. First tell me what each of them can do." Drucker then pointed out that it probably was no coincidence that these presidents had two of the most effective teams of the twentieth century.

Has No Fear of Strong Subordinates:

Drucker's ideal leader knows that he or she is responsible for the well-being of the organization. As such, asserts Drucker, he or she is not afraid of strength in associates and subordinates. Misleaders are fearful; they always go in for purges. But an effective leader wants strong associates; he encourages them, pushes them, indeed glories in them. Because he holds himself ultimately responsible for the mistakes of his associates and subordinates, he also sees the triumphs of his associates and subordinates as his triumphs, rather than as threats.

"A leader may be personally vain—as General MacArthur was to an almost pathological degree. Or he may be personally humble—both Lincoln and Truman were so almost to the point of having inferiority complexes. But all three wanted able, independent, self-assured people around them; they encouraged their associates and subordinates, praising and promoting them. So did a very different person: Dwight 'Ike' Eisenhower, when supreme commander in Europe."

Earns Trust via Consistency:

"The final requirement of effective leadership is to earn trust," wrote Drucker. "When one abandons trust one loses his or her followers, making effective leadership impossible . . . to trust a leader, it is not necessary to like him. Nor is it necessary to agree with him. Trust is the conviction that the leader means what he says . . . a leader's actions and a leader's professed beliefs must be congruent, or at least compatible. Effective leadership—and again this is very old wisdom—is not based on being clever; it is based primarily on being consistent."

Prepare for Tomorrow's Leaders:
Drucker knew that leadership development was a key to any company's future. Drucker took the long view of things, and urged managers to do the same. He felt that too many leaders ran their companies based on the companies' short-term stock prices. Drucker once wrote that many companies owe their leadership position to activities undertaken by people who died a generation ago.

Drucker also felt that every leader had to plan for his or her successor: "The gravest indictment of a leader is for the organization to collapse as soon as he leaves or dies, as happened in Russia the moment Stalin died and as happens all too often in companies. An effective leader knows the ultimate test of leadership is to create human energies and human vision."

The Critical Factors

Just as there are "no leadership qualities," there is no one critical factor. "Leadership is doing the right things," and that entails many factors. We do know that Drucker's ideal leader had the following traits and habits:

Possesses character and courage: these are two of the most fundamental characteristics of a leader.

Creates a clear mission: a leader paints a clear picture of the finish line.

Instills loyalty: a leader understands that loyalty is a two-way street.

Focuses on strength: a leader makes "strengths effective and weaknesses irrelevant."

Does not fear strong subordinates: their successes are your successes.

Is consistent: leadership is not a function of being clever, it is based on consistency.

Develops tomorrow's leaders: the best leaders understand that it is their responsibility to develop leaders who will guide their organization in the years ahead.

Chapter 10

Drucker on Welch

"Jack Welch was, in many ways, a natural. But neither of his predecessors were. They had to learn it the hard way . . . and they learned it. Reg Jones [Welch's predecessor] was the ablest manager, that's the wrong word, the most attractive manager, simply as a human being."

One of the things that struck me about Drucker during our interview was his ability to jump from one topic to another in the blink of an eye. That happened many times, but it was never more entertaining than when Drucker would vault from Alfred Sloan to the great pyramids to the selection of Jack Welch—all in the blink of an eye.

Right after telling me how Sloan "created the professional manager," he told me how he was always being asked who he believed to be the greatest manager in history. "You know my answer?" he asked expectantly.

I fell into the trap and suggested Sloan. I wasn't even in the right millennium.

"The greatest manager of all time," he said uninterrupted, "was the man who conceived, designed, and built—totally unprecedented—the first pyramid . . . no manager I am in knowledge of could possibly accomplish what this fellow did. We don't know how many thousands of people worked for him. They could only work in the short months of spring plowing and fall harvesting. . . .There were many thousands [of workers]; they had to house them, to feed them, to prevent epidemics. You could not start—the pyramid is a tomb—until the pharaoh ascended the throne. And it had to be ready when he died, and most of those were short-lived if only because tuberculosis was endemic. And he accomplished it. Nobody could possibly do that today. It's one of the great mysteries . . . the Egyptians had no numerals. The budget alone must have been impossible," he concluded playfully.

From that story he moved to a more serious discussion of naturals and quickly pivoted to Jack Welch. Although I did not realize it at the time, what he was about to tell me was more than he had ever said publicly about Jack Welch and the GE he inherited when he took over.

In discussing Welch, Drucker made an exception to his rule of not discussing his clients—something he had told me in writing he would not do. In fact, he discussed GE at length and made comparisons between Jack Welch and his predecessor, Reginald Jones, who served as GE's chairman from 1972 to 1981.

Even though few managers under the age of fifty remember Reg Jones (Reg was his nickname), especially when compared to CEO celebrity Jack Welch, Drucker launched into a lengthy discourse about what he accomplished at GE before Welch took over. That prompted me to ask him who he believed was the better manager. Surprisingly, Drucker told me that he felt Jones had qualities that Welch lacked, something that he had never said publicly (before or since). Here is the exact excerpt from that taped conversation:

Drucker: The decency of that man [Jones] was remarkable.... Within GE, Welch was respected and feared, Jones was loved.

Krames: Which is better? [I meant who was the better leader, Welch, who was "respected and feared," or Jones, who was "loved."]

Drucker: Bluntly, Jones ... but Welch would have been very frustrated to have been GE's general manager in the seventies, when GE was basically ... retrenching is the wrong word ... but, defensive. What Reg Jones left to Welch were two things: first, GE was ready to go on the offensive because Jones had restructured it. And Jones was the first one to realize the potential of GE Finance. That was Jones.

And second, that goes back to the fifties. Welch inherited that enormous supply of trained executives which began ... you probably do know that I was one of the founders of Crotonville. And this began really with Crotonville, the systematic development of managers that goes back to Ralph Cordiner.

Some history here: the fuel that made GE the growth engine it became under Welch was GE Capital, its financial services arm. In 2000, for example, it delivered more than $5 billion of the company's operating income (more than 40 percent of the total). Drucker credits Welch's predecessor with starting the financial services business that mushroomed into GE Capital: "Jones realized the potential of GE Finance, which up until then was primarily focused on financing GE's product divisions. Jones began the expansion into finance group services. I can say that clearly because to a large extent I worked with him on that…he saw clearly that services was an area of expansion," said Drucker.

Without financial services, implied Drucker, the story of Jack Welch as CEO superstar may never have been written.

I wondered what was behind Drucker's detailed monologue on Welch. He knew I had edited and/or written more than half a dozen books on Welch, so perhaps he thought it best to speak in the "language" of the leader I knew best.

In hindsight, however, I believe it had more to do with his (Drucker's) legacy. He had spent five decades working behind the scenes helping to make GE one of the most admired and emulated companies in the world, but he had received little of the credit. I remembered what Drucker told me in our first hour together: "The client pays for the consultant's mistake."

What remained unsaid was the other side of the equation: the consultant gets no credit when the company does well. It was no secret that GE was among the world's most successful companies of the past fifty years; however the extent of Drucker's influence on the company was not known.

Few would argue that Drucker had a significant impact on GE. But other than Welch crediting him for a couple of his best moves (for example, which businesses to divest), Drucker received little public acknowledgment for what he had done at GE.

Drucker had not sought trophies or accolades throughout his career, but there is evidence that his legacy was foremost on his mind in the last years of his life. Why else would he agree to my lengthy interview, knowing I intended to write a book on him, and then invite another author to write a book about him as well, something closer to a biography that would be published after his death?*

This was out of character for Drucker, and I remembered what he had said earlier in his career: "One of the secrets of keeping young is not to give interviews but to stick to one's work—and that's what I'm doing. Sorry, I am not available."

Suddenly he had become available.

While he had more humility than most anyone I have ever met, it would be perfectly natural that he would want to be remembered for his far-reaching contributions to a discipline he

---

* Drucker called Elizabeth Haas Edersheim, author of *McKinsey's Marvin Bower*, asking her to write a book on him. The result was *The Definitive Drucker*, a book published about a year after Drucker's death.

helped to establish, and its effects on one of the world's great companies.

The Drucker-GE-Welch Connection

First a bit of history: Drucker and General Electric had long, deep roots. Drucker had been a consultant to GE since the early 1950s. In 1951, then GE CEO Ralph Cordiner assembled an impressive team that included Drucker to find ways to enhance GE's management effectiveness. The team researched dozens of other companies, reviewed personnel records of two thousand GE employees, did time and motion studies of GE executives, and interviewed hundreds of GE managers.

Having little faith in innovative management thinking—"a manager is a manager is a manager," opined CEO Cordiner— the GE CEO commissioned Drucker and others to write a manual that would take the guesswork out of any management challenge, situation, or problem.

The end result of this huge management exercise was something called the Blue Books, a five-volume, 3,463-page management bible. Drucker and others had attempted to write a sort of owner's manual for GE's managers.

However, according to Noel Tichy (noted management professor, consultant, and author), who headed up GE's Crotonville training university during Welch's early years as chairman, several of Welch's key concepts sounded as if they could have come right out of the Blue Books. Tichy wrote in his book on

Welch, "Buried in endless pages of stultifying elaborate prescriptions are such powerful concepts as management by objectives," which was a Drucker invention, "as well as the most revolutionary ideas Welch would later espouse."

Tichy went on to give an example of these earlier thinkers' influence on Welch: "The discussion of decentralization, for instance [excerpted from the Blue Books], sounds a lot like Welch's principle of speed," wrote Tichy. "A minimum of supervision, a minimum of time delays in decision making, a maximum of competitive agility, and thus maximum service to customers and profits to the company." Cordiner founded Crotonville* "to indoctrinate [GE] managers in the new [Blue Book] principles," he added.

Drucker was brought on by Cordiner as a cofounder of Crotonville, and Drucker told me that Crotonville played a key role in supplying GE with a strong management bench for decades—right into the Welch years that started in 1981.

In 1956 some four thousand GE professionals and managers took what was called the Professional Business Management Course (a rigorous thirteen-week program in which participants were cut off from the outside world). In the morning session, lectures were given by top government officials,

---

* Crotonville was so successful that it sparked imitators in the United States and abroad—including IBM's Sands Point School and Hitachi Institute of Management Development in Japan. The Crotonville facility was renamed the John F. Welch Leadership Development Center at Crotonville in 2001.

sociologists, and economists. By the end of the decade the number of managers who took the program increased sixfold, to a cumulative total of twenty-five thousand managers, which constituted more than 10 percent of the GE workforce. That degree of commitment to executive training and development was later amplified by Welch in his Work-Out and Six Sigma initiatives, asserted William Rothschild, a senior corporate strategist from GE. But in the 1950s this type of executive training was totally unprecedented.

What Welch Inherited

Drucker continued his story uninterrupted: "I was one of three founders—the other two [were] CEO of GE [Ralph Cordiner] and the man who brought me into GE as a consultant. He was Harold Smiddy, who had been the senior partner of Booz Allen and Hamilton and then joined GE as head of management consulting . . . he was the architect of the reorganization of GE,* to which I was the main consultant in the late forties, really early fifties. . . . Welch had an enormous supply of trained, tested, and focused executives. Without those two [Cordiner and Smiddy], Welch couldn't have done it."

I was thunderstruck. *Without those two, Welch couldn't have done it?* That contradicted every book I had edited or written on

---

* The reorganization Drucker referred to was a sweeping initiative to decentralize GE, pushing decision making down into the organization.

Welch the previous dozen years. Each of those seven books painted Welch as a CEO-savior who had reinvented an aging industrial dinosaur sinking under the weight of its own bureaucracy. And here was Drucker, longtime consultant to Welch and GE, painting a very different picture of the Welch years.

He depicted GE circa 1980 as a company ready to take off, as if it were some giant slot machine that had been primed to deliver a huge payout to the next person who arrived with a roll of quarters.

The relationship between Drucker and Welch is a fascinating one. While Welch credits Drucker for his "number one, number two" strategy (which held that any firm that could not be a market leader should get out of that market), there are other tactics and pages from the Welch playbook that appeared to have originated with Drucker.

For example, in 1984 Welch decided to sell off its Housewares Division, the part of the company that many felt defined GE. Welch knew that Housewares was a mature business and did not play well to GE's strengths. Drucker told me that the decision to sell off that division was decided in the same room in which we sat that day. "He credits me for that decision," said Drucker offhandedly.

Given their relationship, I wanted to be sure that I was not misinterpreting Drucker's characterization of GE under Welch. I found it hard to believe that the CEO widely regarded as the best of his generation—the one crowned Manager of the Century—succeeded because of actions taken decades earlier by

Drucker and others. So I asked him straight out: "Dr. Drucker, are you saying that GE was ready, ripe for someone like Welch?"

His answer only added more fuel to the fire: *"More than that,"* Drucker shot back. That's when Drucker went into the discussion of GE's financial services business, how it had been started before Welch took over.

What do the facts say?

In his memoir, *Jack: Straight from the Gut*, Welch reported that in 1978, three years *before* he took over, GE Capital had $5 billion in assets. However, Welch's intense focus on services transformed the company from a manufacturing giant into a services juggernaut. By 2000, Welch had negotiated or green-lighted hundreds of acquisitions for GE Capital, and the unit had exploded in size. By Welch's last year as CEO, GE Capital had skyrocketed to $370 billion in assets and contributed more than 41 percent of the company's total income.

In retrospect, the facts, to borrow a favorite Drucker word, are "murky." Reg Jones started GE down the path of financial services, which played such an important part in Welch's playbook, but Welch invested and grew this business beyond almost anyone's imagination.

The Right Man for the Future

Drucker ended this part of the conversation by telling me, "Jones picked Welch because he was the right person for the business plan. He was not the right person to run GE ... to run Reg Jones's GE, that was another man ... a close friend of mine, who was the other man in the running ... who bowed out voluntarily, because he said I am the wrong man for the future, I am the right man for the present, but you need a man for the future. He was executive vice chairman, a vice president. A year after Welch took over he bowed out voluntarily, on this sofa." (Drucker pointed to the sofa behind me. I took that to mean that the executive made the decision to end his bid for the chairmanship while talking to Drucker in Drucker's home.)

When the announcement came that Welch would succeed Reg Jones, *The Wall Street Journal* reported that GE had decided to replace "a legend with a live wire." Ironically, when it was all over, Jack Welch would be the modern-day CEO most associated with the word *legend*.

When he decided to write his memoir, *Jack: Straight from the Gut*, publishers fell over themselves to bid on it. The winner was Warner Books, which paid the huge sum of $7.1 million for the rights to publish his book. At that time, it was the largest advance ever paid for a nonfiction book, with a single exception: Pope John Paul II's *Crossing the Threshold of Hope*, which received $8.5 million. (Since then, Hillary Clinton and Bill Clinton have received $8 million and $12 million, respectively, and Alan Greenspan has received $8.5 million.)

Reconciling the Accounts

As one who spent years editing and writing some seven books on Welch, I would be less than responsible if I left the discussion incomplete. Drucker felt strongly that Welch was dealt a winning hand with a strong business plan in place. However, there are a number of extenuating points that need to be made in order to complete the picture.

First, despite his assertion that the table was set for Welch when he took over, Drucker told me that Welch was a born leader: "Jack Welch was, in many ways, a natural. . . . Welch's great strength is his ability to ask what needs to be done, to focus on the priorities, and delegate everything else." He also knew how critical it was to focus on priorities and not get distracted: "So for five years—the first five years—his priority was to restructure GE," said Drucker, "and then he asked again what needs to be done and set a new priority. And the last priority was to restructure GE around information."

Last, it should be noted that Drucker praised Welch, not only to me, but in his books. In *Management Challenges for the 21st Century*, Drucker pointed out that "since Welch took over as CEO in 1981, GE has created more wealth than any company in the world."

He credited Welch with the way he organized his company around information, a critical factor for organizations in the knowledge-based society: "The main factor for [Welch's success] was that GE organized the same information about the performance of every one of its business units differently for different purposes. It kept traditional financial and marketing reporting, the way most companies appraise their businesses every year or so. But the same data were also organized for long-range strategy, that is, to show unexpected successes and failures, but also to show where actual events differed substantially from what was expected."

Drucker on Welch

The key takeaway from this chapter involves the issue of time frame and leadership. Before Drucker explained to me that Welch was the right person for the future of GE, it was easy to think of leaders in two dimensions. That entailed hiring the best person for the job without taking time frame into account. Drucker once said, "There is no such thing as a good man. Good for what is the question." Drucker's discussion about Welch instilled in me an understanding of the fit between managers, organization, and time frame. When Welch was hired, he was the right leader for the *future* of GE, not the GE of yesterday or today. When important posts are to be filled, it is imperative to look past immediate needs. Welch would have been the wrong leader for 1971, and perhaps for 2001 (the year he retired). But he was the right leader to perform the massive corporate surgery that was needed in the 1980s and 1990s.

Chapter 11

Life-and-death Decisions

"Promotion decisions are what I call 'life and death decisions for managers.'"

I n the 1980s, after the publication of *The One Minute Manager* (Blanchard and Johnson) and *In Search of Excellence* (Peters and Waterman), some overly eager business authors were hailing the coming of a new organization that would bear little resemblance to the organization that preceded it. This was during an empowerment movement that promised to turn rigid command-and-control organizations upside down, flattening the traditional organizational structure like a pancake.

Drucker, however, understood the false promise: "A few years ago...there was all this talk about the death of hierarchy," he wrote in 2002. "We would all be one happy crew, sailing together on the same ship. Well, it hasn't happened, and isn't about to happen, for one simple reason: When the ship is going down you don't call a caucus—you give a command. There has to be somebody who says, 'enough dithering, this is it.' Without a decision maker you'll never make a decision."

Without a decision maker you'll never make a decision is another classic Druckerism. This chapter is about decisions, not just any decisions but the ones Drucker considered to be most vital to the future of an organization, the ones he started out calling life-and-death decisions.

In this chapter we will examine Drucker's approach and recommendations on people decisions, product decisions, and the other key decisions that stare managers in the face every day.

Life-and-death Decisions Defined

One of the keys to making the right calls on life-and-death decisions is never to delegate them. At first Drucker defined them narrowly, to encompass people decisions (later he would talk of other critical decisions, but not call them life-and-death decisions). But people decisions are almost always life-and-death.

Drucker explained that key hiring and promotion decisions do not happen very often. But when they do, they should be taken very seriously and never rushed: "Few things are less likely to succeed than hasty person decisions. And the same applies to most of the other top-management decisions."

The first life-and-death decisions Drucker wrote of were these:

- Promotion decisions: whom to promote and when

- To fire or demote a manager

- Decisions on the scope and work of a manager's unit (capital investments, for example)

Whom to Promote?

As discussed in chapter 9, Drucker knew early on what he looked for in a leader, for example, integrity, character, and consistency. But those were just the prerequisites. He thought the strongest leaders looked for strengths in others, but did not shy away from their own weaknesses. That's why the most effective leaders make the most strategic people decisions by hiring and promoting people who are strongest in areas in which they are the weakest: "Never try to be an expert if you are not. Build on your strengths and find strong people to do the other necessary tasks," he urged.

This does not mean that you should look for the mistake-free employee. "I would never promote a man into a top level job who had not made mistakes, and big ones at that. Otherwise he is sure to be mediocre," said Drucker.

As for when to promote someone, one clue is to look for someone who is dissatisfied. That is someone who wants to do more. Last, look for someone with a track record. "In the last analysis," explained Drucker, "management is practice. Its essence is not knowing but doing. Its test is not logic but results. Its only authority is performance."

Whom to Fire?

"Any manager or individual who does not perform at a high level should be removed," said Drucker repeatedly. Immaturity in a manager is unacceptable. Those that get caught up in their own egos destroy an organization. Those are the people who think of themselves before the organization, who feel it is more important to be right than do right. Leaders lead by example by living the values of the organization and setting the bar high for themselves and their people. Anything less will sink their division or organization over the long run.

Defining the Scope of Each Job:

It is essential for every one of your direct reports to know what is expected of him or her. There is nothing more wasteful than someone who fritters away time because he or she does not know what to do. It is therefore imperative that a manager set clear objectives and, equally as important, remove any impediments that interfere with the performance of that job. Last, all responsible leaders think of tomorrow's organization. Anything less is irresponsible.

In later books Drucker used the phrase *life-and-death decision* less frequently. However, managerial decision making continued to be a dominant theme in his books. For example, in

Managing for Results (1964), he spoke of the importance of "priority decisions," which we will discuss later in this chapter. Whatever we call them, the most effective executives not only make the right calls more often than the wrong ones, but they get the big ones right most of the time. That is what separates the most effective executives from the also-rans.

Who Makes Life-and-death Decisions?

In two of his key early works,* Drucker made the point that one does not need to have the title of manager in order to make an organization's most critical calls.

In *The Effective Executive*, he asserted: "Throughout every one of our knowledge organizations, we have people who manage no one and are still executives. Rarely indeed do we find a situation such as that in the Viet Nam jungle, where at any moment, a member of the group is called upon to make decisions with life and death impact for the whole."

However, in a knowledge organization it's not only senior managers who make critical decisions—junior people can, and do, make decisions that affect the future of the organization as well. As an example he points to the chemist who "follows one line of inquiry rather than another" and determines the future of the organization. Another example might be a young prod-

---

* *Managing for Results* (1964) and *The Effective Executive* (1967).

uct manager who tweaks an existing product and turns it into the company's most popular new product introduction of the next year.

This type of organization, in which so many people at so many levels can make a substantial contribution, represents a vast departure from the organizations of yesterday, such as the organization of 1918 that Drucker described in chapter 5. That was the corporation with a few senior managers and a large number of unskilled or semiskilled workers below them. In those organizations, only top managers could make life-and-death decisions, as the people below were not equipped to make them. Even if they were, there was no mechanism for them to contribute new ideas to the company. Remember that in Taylor's [scientific management] world, there was "One Best Way" to achieve any task, meaning that no one worker was more talented than any other.

What changed the game was the advent of knowledge workers. "Knowledge work is not defined by its quantity. Nor is it defined by its costs," explains Drucker. "It is defined by results."

Drucker used the term *executives* to refer to those "knowledge workers, managers, or individual professionals who are expected by virtue of their position or their knowledge to make decisions . . . that have significant impact on the performance and results of the whole." Most knowledge workers do not have the chance to alter the future of an organization, since only the most talented can do that. But, he added, in every company there are more people who can change the destiny of an organization than any organization chart ever reveals.

Last, what few grasp is how many people there are, even in the most stagnant or mature businesses, who "have to make decisions of significant and irreversible impact," decisions that resemble those made by top management. "For the authority of knowledge is surely as legitimate as the authority of position," declared Drucker.

However, knowledge is not enough. People only accomplish important things when they are not sidetracked or distracted by meaningless tasks. In Drucker's words: "The people who actually do most of the knowledge and service work in organizations—engineers, teachers, salespeople, nurses, middle managers in general—carry a steadily growing load of business busy work, additional activities that contribute little or no value and that have little or nothing to do with what these people are qualified and paid for."

The Three Officers Rule

The Three Officers Rule is something that Drucker learned from Ralph Cordiner, the GE CEO whom he worked with on the Blue Books and Crotonville. This rule holds that a responsible CEO should identify, within three years of accepting the position, and have available at least three candidates "equal or better than himself" who can succeed him should the need arise. But it isn't only CEOs who need to worry about tomorrow, all managers should.

Explained Drucker: "The first principle of manager development must therefore be the development of the entire management group.... The second principle is that manager development must be dynamic.... It must always focus on the needs of tomorrow.... The job of developing tomorrow's managers is both too big and too important to be considered a special activity. Its performance depends on all factors in the managing of managers: the organization of a man's job and his relationship to his superior and his subordinates; the spirit of the organization; and its organization structure." That activity, ensuring for tomorrow's leaders, is more important in today's talent-scarce organizations, in which the organization needs its best people more than its best people need the organization.

Priority Decisions

In *Managing for Results*, Drucker advanced his thinking on the game-changing decisions that face managers and how they should be prioritized. He explained that no matter how well managed or organized a company is, there are always more opportunities than the resources to exploit them. As a result, there must be "priority decisions, or nothing will get done." Making these decisions will force managers to face the realities of their situation, "its strengths and weaknesses, its opportunities and needs."

"Priority decisions convert good intentions into effective commitments, and insights into action," he wrote. He also suggested that one could tell a great deal about a firm's management by the priorities they set. "Priority decisions bespeak the level of a management's vision and seriousness. They decide basic behavior and strategy."

One of the keys to priority decisions is to know what should *not* be done. He explained that people have few problems setting priorities; however, the larger problem that managers have is deciding on what he called "posteriorities," the things that should not be done. "It cannot be said often enough that one should not postpone; one abandons." This should come as no surprise, since planned abandonment is such a vital part of the Drucker playbook.

He suggests that managers need to be disciplined to walk away from what seemed like a good idea or opportunity: "It's almost always a serious mistake to go back to something no matter how desirable it might have appeared when, sometime back, it had to be postponed."

In other words, don't be afraid to walk away from a deal or product that had been postponed or has failed to yield results despite considerable investment. He felt that managers get too married or too vested in ideas that made sense at one point, but later, when evaluated with a fresh eye, make little sense in light of tomorrow's realities.

That's because "business is society's change agent," as Drucker explained years later, adding the following: "The seemingly most successful business of today is a sham and a failure if it does not create its own and different tomorrow. It must innovate and re-create its products or services but equally the enterprise itself. All other major institutions of society are designed to *conserve* if not to prevent change. *Business alone is designed to innovate* [italics are Drucker's emphasis]. No business will long survive, let alone prosper, unless it innovates successfully."

The key, says Drucker, is to take the company's scarce resources and match them up with the greatest opportunities. Concentrate on those very few products, services, and ideas that are likely to produce the greatest results. Companies that try to do too many things at one time will fail, argued Drucker. "Above all," he explained, "the truly big opportunities—those that realize potential and those that make the future—must receive the resources their potential deserves, even at the price of abandoning immediate, seemingly safe, but small ventures."

In 2004 he explained that one of the biggest traps for managers is when one manager is urged to keep at something when there is almost no chance for success. That manager often gives in to peer pressure and gives it his all to get something to work (it can be a new product or service, a variation on a product, a new process, et cetera). That's why Drucker urged, "Don't tell me what you're doing, tell me what you *stopped* doing."

Life-and-death Decisions

There are no decisions more important than people decisions. Drucker never forgot the lessons he had gleaned from
Alfred Sloan. "Executives spend more time on managing
people and making people decisions than on anything
else—and they should," insisted Drucker. "No decision is as
long lasting in its consequences or as difficult to unmake." He
added that most executives make bad people decisions, with
a batting average no better than .333: one third of new hires
are good ones; one third are "minimally effective," and one
third are disasters. Sloan's people selection over the long run,
contended Drucker, was flawless, because he made every
key management decision personally. And if it appears that
Sloan micromanaged hiring decisions, he should be forgiven,
simply because of how important his selections were to the
success of GM.

   After people decisions come the priority decisions: how
to allocate resources. The key is to put your best people
where they can make the greatest impact. Organizations
that have their A players dealing with the mundane, such as
turf battles, are mismanaged. Last, don't let "investments in
managerial ego" get in the way of abandoning projects that
have been postponed or sidetracked.

Chapter 12

The Strategic Drucker

"Without understanding the mission, the objectives and the strategy of the enterprise, managers cannot be managed, organizations cannot be designed, managerial jobs cannot be made productive."

The story is now part of Peter Drucker lore. The original title for Drucker's 1964 book *Managing for Results* was *Business Strategies*. However, back then, in the 1960s, *strategy* was not a term people used very much.

When Drucker and his publisher tested the title *Business Strategies* with managers, consultants, professors, and booksellers, they were talked out of the title. "Strategy, we were told again and again, belongs to military or perhaps to political campaigns but not to business." Drucker pointed out that the 1952 edition of the *Concise Oxford Dictionary* still defined strategy as

"Generalship; the art of war; management of an army or armies in a campaign."

Of course, within a decade management strategy had become one of the most popular and most studied aspects of management and business.

Purpose and Objectives First

To Drucker, strategy, like everything else in management, is a thinking person's game. It isn't arrived at by following some rigid set of rules but by thinking through various aspects of the business.

It all starts with objectives. "Only a clear definition of the mission makes possible clear and realistic business objectives. It is the foundation for priorities, strategies, plans and work assignments. It is the starting point for the design of managerial jobs, and, above all, for the design of managerial structures. Structure follows strategy. Strategy determines what the key activities are in a given business. And strategy requires knowing what our business is and what it should be."

Drucker also explained that "nothing may seem simpler or more obvious than to answer what a company's business is. A steel mill makes steel, a railroad runs to carry freight and passengers.... Actually 'what is our business?' is almost always a difficult question which can be answered only after hard thinking and studying. And the right answer is usually anything but obvious."

Thinking back to Drucker's Law, no strategy can be created without the customer, for it is the customer who defines business purpose. And "therefore the question 'what is our business?' can be answered only by looking at the business from the outside, from the point of view of the customer and the market. What the customer sees, thinks, believes and wants at any given time must be accepted by management as an objective fact deserving to be taken as seriously" as any hard data collected from salespeople, accountants, or engineers, contended Drucker.

Drucker claimed that the single most important cause of business failure can be attributed to management's failure to ask the question "what is our business?" in a "clear and sharp form." And it isn't only when a company is starting out that the question should be asked, or when the company is in trouble. "On the contrary," Drucker wrote, "to raise the question and to study it thoroughly is most needed when a business is successful. For then failure to raise it may result in rapid decline."

Drucker uses American Telephone and Telegraph Company of the early twentieth century as a company that got it right. Long before it became popular to associate the word *service* with business,* the president of American Telephone came up with

---

* One other early company that stressed the theme of service was IBM: We sell service was one of the slogans Thomas J. Watson, Sr., hung on the wall.

the following definition of his business: "Our business is service."

Drucker admitted that that sounded obvious, but it was anything but at the time. First, American Telephone was a monopoly, so it wasn't as if their customers could buy their competitor's product. However, that definition of the business meant a "radical innovation in business policy. It required intensive training, or indoctrination," in Drucker's parlance, of the company's entire workforce and a PR campaign focused on service.

It also required a "financial policy which assumed the company had to give service wherever there was a demand, and that it was a management's job to find the needed capital and earn a return on it," added Drucker. "In retrospect all these things are obvious; but it took well over a decade to work them out." Drucker then poses the question, "Would we have gone through the New Deal period without a serious attempt at telephone nationalization but for the careful analysis of its business that the Telephone Company made [in the early 1900s]?"

A Twenty-First-Century Example

It is easy to regard the question "what is our business?" as one that belongs in dusty old management textbooks that no one reads. What manager doesn't know what business he or she is in? However, a contemporary example will illustrate the power and longevity of Drucker's "what is our business?" tenet.

After studying scores of companies and success stories, I discovered one modern-day company that adhered most closely to Drucker's classical principles of management: online retailer Amazon.com.

Like many great start-ups, Amazon has an incredible company story. According to company lore, founder Jeff Bezos hatched the original business plan in a Chevy Blazer during a car trip with his wife from Fort Worth, Texas, to Bellevue, Washington.

Defining a Twenty-First-Century Business

Jeff Bezos worked in the computer science field before entering the world of investment banking, first with Bankers Trust Company and later D. E. Shaw & Company. The latter was an edgy, quantitative hedge fund that garnered much interest for its innovative trading techniques. Bezos excelled at each of his jobs. In 1994, CEO David Shaw handed Bezos what turned out to be the assignment of a lifetime: to study and analyze potential business opportunities on the Internet.

It was then that Bezos discovered an amazing statistic: Internet usage was growing at an incredible 2,300 percent a year. Bezos knew that was no ordinary number: "You have to keep in mind that human beings aren't good at understanding exponential growth," he said. "It's just not something we see in our everyday lives . . . things don't grow this fast outside of Petri dishes. It just doesn't happen." He also said, "When something is growing 2,300 percent a year, you have to move fast. A sense of urgency becomes your greatest asset."

Bezos then compiled a list of twenty potential products that could be sold online, including music and office supplies. However, books rose to the top of the list after Bezos learned that the industry was so fragmented, with more than three million books in print and tens of thousands of publishers. Even the industry's number one publisher, Random House, controlled less than 10 percent of the market.

Incredibly, in September of 1994, Bezos attended an introductory four-day book-selling course in Portland, Oregon, sponsored by the American Booksellers' Association. Included in the less-than-thrilling course curricula were seminars on "Developing a Business Plan"; "Ordering, Receiving, Returning"; and "Inventory Management."

Those were not the only lessons taught that week, however. The president of the American Booksellers' Association delivered an inspiring story about customer service when he told the anecdote of how a customer's car somehow became covered in dirt parked next to his bookstore. The customer was so upset that he offered to hand wash the car at his home across town. That story stayed with Bezos, who vowed to make customer service the "cornerstone of Amazon.com."

Amazon.com was started in 1994, went live in 1995, and went public in 1997. One interesting fact about Amazon was that it was not the first online bookseller (or even the second or third). It followed clbooks.com, books.com, and wordsworth.

com (wordsworth.com beat Amazon by almost two full years). However, Amazon was the best conceived and most customer-centric from the outset, posing a real threat to traditional brick-and-mortar stores like Barnes & Noble and Borders.

Bezos's continual focus on the customer played a vital role in helping the company keep its edge. In its first years of business, Bezos reportedly met with his people every three months to remind them that great customer service was the key to the company's success.

One of the other success factors was how its founder defined the business. In the early years Bezos could have easily answered the Drucker question "what is our business?" with the answer "an online bookstore." After all, that's exactly what it was in its first years.

In Bezos's first letter to shareholders he foretold the future of his firm: "We set out to offer customers something they simply could not get any other way, and *began* serving them with books."

In his second letter to shareholders (the 1998 letter), the Amazon CEO made this assertion: "We are working to build a place where tens of millions of customers can come to find and discover *anything* they might want to buy online. It is truly Day 1 for the Internet and, if we execute our business plan well, it remains Day 1 for Amazon.com."

We now know that Bezos figured out what the business "should be"—thus answering a classic Drucker question—as early as December 1996. At a company retreat that included all

Amazon employees, the discussion was focused on how the company was going to expand the company's product line beyond books, so reports Robert Spector, author of the book *Amazon.com: Get Big Fast*.

One Amazon manager summed it up: "It was obvious from the beginning that Amazon couldn't stay in books and have margins that anyone would be happy with long-term."

Had Bezos defined his company more narrowly he would have limited its business model and ability to execute his broad product diversification strategy. Long before the company yielded any profits, he envisioned an online juggernaut where people could buy "*anything* online." Within a few years the company expanded its offerings to include music CDs, DVDs, MP3s, computer software, video games, tools, electronics, clothes, furniture, food, toys, et cetera.

Rather than define the company by its product line, Bezos stressed customer experience ("obsess over customers") and created a "community of customers" as two keys to the company's success. Unlike in traditional bookstores, an Amazon.com customer could get personally involved by leaving book reviews and rating the books they read. Authors were also encouraged to get involved by answering a series of questions that would be posted on their book page on the site.

From a publisher's perspective, these innovations represented a huge breakthrough. Before Amazon.com, editors and marketing managers had no mechanism to get feedback directly from readers. Now publishers could read reviews of their books as well as all of their competitors straight from the ultimate consumer.

Also, Amazon rated every book based on an hourly sales ranking, providing publishers with real-time data on how their books were selling. Before the Amazon ratings there were printed best-seller lists, but those lists included only a tiny fraction of all books published. Amazon.com delivered the entire universe of books, with real-time information, to publishers, authors, readers, the media, and anyone else who loved books.

A CEO in Drucker's Image

Despite all the talk of a "new economy" and how "the Internet changes everything," Amazon.com was built on classic business concepts that could have come straight out of the Drucker playbook, as we will see in the pages that follow.

Bezos is a natural, but founding and growing an online business in the dawn of the Internet was a daunting task, especially a company that would quickly become one of the most recognized online brands in the world.

In the mid-to-late 1990s, Bezos called the World Wide Web the World Wide Wait (dial-up Internet was maddeningly slow back then), and people were afraid to put their credit card information "out there," on the Web. There were plenty of roadblocks for any new online business to overcome in those first years of Internet commerce.

Despite the obstacles, Bezos succeeded in making sure that

people who visited his Web site had a great experience. He also did all of the other things that Drucker regarded as essential to ensuring the long-term health of the company. He was not only a smart chief executive but, more important, an *effective* one.

Following Drucker's Playbook

From his first years in the business Jeff Bezos understood that the firm's objectives, current and future, are not "abstractions" (Drucker's word). He knew that he needed to grow the company, and that growth had to be more profitable than the razor-thin margins afforded by the book business.

Drucker said, "It is . . . irrational not to plan for growth . . . every business needs a growth goal, a growth strategy, and ways to distinguish healthy growth from fat and cancer." He also asserted: "Organization must be reviewed as the business changes. Is division into different components still likely to advance the economic performance of the company as a whole? Or is it likely to make the component's results look good at the expense of the overall company?"

We now know that Bezos thought through these critical Drucker questions while the business was in its infancy. He figured out what the business should be today (books), and tomorrow (most everything else!).

Let's take a closer look at what Bezos did—how he communicated his vision and strategy—and compare it to Drucker's writings and teachings. A close look at the passages that follow reveals a modern-day CEO who knew how to ask the right questions at critical times and, just as important, take decisive action to make sure that nothing—from competitors to new technologies to an out-of-date business plan—would derail the company as he grew it from nothing into the world's number one online retailer.

Obsess over Customers

Drucker: "It is the customer who determines what a business is. For it is the customer, and he alone, who through being willing to pay for a good or a service, converts economic resources into wealth, things into goods. What the business thinks it produces is not of first importance—especially not to the future of the business and to its success. What the customer thinks he is buying, what he considers 'value,' is decisive—it determines what a business is, what it produces and whether it will prosper. The customer is the foundation of a business and keeps it in existence. He alone gives employment."

Bezos: "From the beginning, our focus has been on offering our customers compelling value ... we set out to offer customers something they simply could not get any other way, and began serving them with books. We brought them much more selection than was possible in a physical store, and presented it in a useful, easy-to-search, and easy-to-browse format in a store open 365 days a year, 24 hours a day. We maintained a dogged focus on improving the shopping experience.... We dramatically lowered prices, further increasing customer value. Word of mouth remains the most powerful customer acquisition tool we have, and we are grateful for the trust our customers have placed in us."

"It's All About the Long Term"

Drucker: "There is one more major factor in every management problem, every decision, every action—not, properly speaking, a fourth function of management, but an additional dimension: time. Management always has to consider both the present and the long-range future."

Bezos: "It's all about the long term" became a catchphrase in Jeff Bezos's annual letter to shareholders, starting with his very first letter in 1997. Under that heading, Bezos wrote, "We believe that a fundamental measure of our success will be the shareholder value we create over the *long term* [emphasis added] ... our decisions have consistently reflected this focus ... because of our emphasis on the long term, we may make decisions and weigh tradeoffs differently than some companies."

Don't Let Wall Street Run the Company

Drucker: He warned managers that leadership in any market is fleeting and that today becomes obsolete almost immediately. He also urged managers never to manage their companies by that day's Dow Jones average (meaning don't let the short-term stock price influence key management decisions).

Bezos: He vowed to "make investment decisions in light of long-term *market leadership* [emphasis added] considerations rather than short-term profitability considerations or short-term Wall Street reactions." In 2000 he added, "As the famed investor Benjamin Graham said, "In the short term, the stock market is a voting machine; in the long term, it's a weighing machine.... We're a company that wants to be weighed, and over time, we will be—over the long term, all companies are."

The Wrong Decision Is Better Than No Decision

Drucker: "Priority decisions must be made 'deliberately and consciously'... it is better to make the wrong decision and carry it out than to shirk the job as unpleasant and painful, and, as a result, to allow the accidents of the business to set priorities by default."

Bezos: He was once asked about Amazon's investment decisions that had gone awry. "You do enough of these things and you're going to bet wrong," shot back the Amazon founder. However, if senior management doesn't "make some significant mistakes in our investments . . . then we won't be doing a good job for our shareholders because we won't be swinging for the fences. You should *expect* mistakes."

Take Risks That Benefit Tomorrow

Drucker: "Of course innovation is risky. But so is stepping into the supermarket for a loaf of bread. All economic activity is by definition 'high risk.' And defending yesterday—that is, not innovating—is far more risky than making tomorrow."

Bezos: From the beginning, Bezos was not afraid to take calculated risks: "We will make bold rather than timid investment decisions where we see a sufficient probability of gaining market leadership advantages. Some of these investments will pay off, others will not, and we will have learned another valuable lesson in either case." In 2000 he added: "Many of you have heard me talk about the 'bold bets' that we as a company have made and will continue to make—these bold bets have included everything from our investment in digital and wireless technologies, to our decision to invest in smaller e-commerce companies. . . ."

Objectives Represent the Strategy

Drucker: "Objectives must be defined from 'what our business is, what it will be, and what it should be.' They are not abstractions. They are the action commitments through which the mission of the business is to be carried out, and the standards against which performance is to be measured. Objectives, in other words, represent the fundamental strategy of a business."

Bezos: He has consistently laid out the objectives of the firm: "Our vision is to use this platform to build Earth's most customer-centric company, a place where customers can come to find and discover anything and everything they might want to buy online. We won't do so alone, but together with what will be thousands of partners of all sizes. We'll listen to customers, invent on their behalf, and personalize the store for each of them, all while working hard to continue to earn their trust."

Grow Through Strategic Alliances

Drucker: He felt that organizations that wanted to get access to new markets or technologies should seek out strategic alliances via partnerships, joint ventures, or minority participations instead of buying companies outright: "Such entities, rather than a traditional model of a parent company with wholly owned subsidiaries, are increasingly becoming the models for growth, especially in the global economy."

Bezos: He made investments in companies like drugstore. com, Sotheby's, HomeGrocer.com. However, its biggest game changer was what Amazon called zShops, the equivalent of an online shopping mall. This made Amazon's millions of customers accessible to thousands of merchants who paid monthly transaction fees to Amazon. This was a key Bezos strategy: "We don't really care whether we sell something through zShops, or sell something directly ourselves; it is sort of a wash for us. You can't sell everything on your own. You need to band together with third parties."

The results are incontrovertible. Clearly the Bezos strategy of managing for the long term paid off. A decade after the company went public (at a split-adjusted price of $1.50 per share), the company's revenues topped $13 billion. Amazon.com's share price hovers at around $85 and the company is worth more than $33 billion—more than General Motors and Xerox combined. The stock doubled in value in 1997 and shows no signs of slowing down. The stock is selling at more than ninety times its earnings, which means that investors are extremely optimistic about the company's future.

The Strategic Drucker

Strategy begins with asking the basic question of what is the business. "Objectives must be defined from 'what our business is, what it will be, and what it should be,'" explained Drucker. He also points out, "Defining the purpose and mission of the business is difficult, painful, and risky. But it alone enables a business to set objectives, to develop strategies, to concentrate its resources, and to go to work. It alone enables a business to be managed for performance."

"Structure follows strategy. Strategy determines what the key activities are in a given business. And strategy requires knowing what our business is and what it should be." Drucker also explained that "the right structure does not guarantee results." However, the wrong structure will make attaining the goals of the enterprise impossible. The structure of an organization "has to be such that it highlights the results that are truly meaningful; that is, the results that are relevant to the idea of the business, its excellence, its priorities, and its opportunities."

Chapter 13

The Fourth Information Revolution

"A new Information Revolution is well under way. It has started in business enterprise, and with business information. But it will surely engulf all institutions. It will radically change the meaning of information for both enterprises and individuals."

One of Drucker's strengths was his ability to place any event into a context that most anyone could understand. A. G. Lafley, Chairman and CEO of Procter & Gamble, who worked closely with Drucker for years, said, "[One] characteristic that made Peter extraordinary was his gift for reducing complexity to simplicity. His curiosity was insatiable, and he never stopped asking questions." Lafley pointed out that Drucker regarded himself as a social ecologist, because in making sense of the world, he didn't restrict his thoughts to business but also included history, anthropology, art, literature, sociology, and economics, among other subjects.

Drucker owes his broad view of the world, at least in part, to his childhood and early years. He was raised in a Viennese household in which artists, politicians, and a variety of creative types and intellectuals socialized most evenings with Drucker's parents, who also knew Sigmund Freud. Drucker himself was introduced to Freud when he was eight years old (see the Epilogue for more on Drucker's early years).

His classical education and his early jobs as newspaper journalist and editor in Frankfurt, Germany, and then as a banker in London put Drucker in touch with all sorts of people who would help widen his view of the world. His spot-on predictions about Hitler and the Holocaust and the German-Soviet pact of World War II confirmed his prophetic abilities.

Drucker became particularly able to recognize the key turning points of history, and he examined these from different angles at different times in different books. By shifting his angle of vision, he was able to show the impact of an event or invention on managers and organizations while allowing readers to trace the evolution of his thoughts on a great many topics.

The best example of this is how Drucker chronicled the ever-changing role of information and knowledge, and its impact on organizations and society. He explored the big picture of how information—its use and application—has defined different eras throughout history. He has covered information technology and its effect on management decision making, for better or worse, and surprisingly, for many years Drucker made a compelling case for worse.

He has also documented the information that managers receive and how they receive it and how it affected their approach to their jobs, how they view their companies and the outside world. He also shows how information has transformed the DNA of organizations and society as a whole. This chapter is devoted to Drucker's views on the ever-changing role of information on organizations and society and how it changed over the fifty-plus years that he prolifically, and prophetically, wrote of it.

Remember that Drucker did not revise his books.* There are no second or third editions of *Concept of the Corporation* or *The Practice of Management* or any other Drucker book. Instead, when he had a new idea he wrote a new book, often retracing old territory but from a different vantage point. To understand his thinking on a key topic and how it changed over the years, one is forced to read several of his key books and compare and contrast his assertions and predictions.

Early Views

In 1954, in *The Practice of Management*, Drucker wrote of information in the context of using it to enhance an executive's productivity: "Each manager should have the information he needs

---

* Drucker and his publisher, however, did repackage earlier chapters of his works into later works. One such example is *The Essential Drucker*.

to measure his own performance and should receive it soon enough to make any changes necessary for the desired results. And this information should go to the manager himself, and not to his superior. It should be the means of self-control, not a tool of control from above." He added, "Only if he has all the information regarding his operations can he fully be held accountable for results."

Note how Drucker thought of information when he wrote of it in the mid-1950s. He regarded it as an *internal* management tool and not as something that would help the manager better understand the outside world, which became a dominant theme in later works.

In *The Effective Executive* (1967), for example, Drucker combined two of his key themes: the limits of machines in aiding decision making and management effectiveness, and the importance of maintaining an outside-in perspective. He explained that the larger companies focus on the wrong things: "And yet the bigger and apparently more successful an organization gets to be, the more will inside events tend to engage the interests, the energies and the abilities of the executive to the exclusion of his real tasks and his effectiveness in the outside."

He added, "The danger is being aggravated today by the advent of the computer and of the new information technology. The computer, being a mechanical moron, can handle only quantifiable data. One can, however, by and large quantify only what goes on inside an organization. . . . The relevant outside events are rarely available in quantifiable form until it is much too late to do anything about them."

Warning managers of the limits and potential perils of machines was a common theme in many of Drucker's works. In his beefiest book, *Management: Tasks, Responsibilities, Practices* (1973), he wrote of the dangers of overreliance on computers: "When the new computer arrives, a frantic search begins to find things for it to do. In the end, it is being used to turn out endless reams of information that nobody wants, nobody needs, and nobody can use. Keeping the tool going becomes an end. As a result, nobody has any information."

Drucker added that organizations need people who ask the key question: "What does top management need in order to make its decisions . . . and not only for today's decisions, but tomorrow's as well."

This is classic Drucker. He never fell in love with technology or any other crutch that managers could fall back on to either think less or dodge the tough questions. But over the years Drucker's views on information—and its relationship to organizations and managers—changed. He would come to view how organizations used information as a genuine game-changer. Those firms that used it to gain a better understanding of the *outside* (for example, customers, the marketplace, and competitors) would have a leg up on those companies that used information only as an internal tool.

The Coming of the New Organization

By the late 1980s Drucker more fully conceptualized the organization of tomorrow by contrasting it with the rigid hierarchies of yesterday. In 1988 he wrote a prescient article that appeared in a *Harvard Business Review* piece titled "The Coming of the New Organization." In the piece Drucker defined the organization of the future by how it leveraged information to gain competitive advantage. To place this emerging organization in context, he described three phases of the corporation.

The first phase took place in the early twentieth century, when industrial barons like J. P. Morgan and Andrew Carnegie cleared the way for professional managers. "This established management as work and task in its own right," explained Drucker.

The second phase organization, which gave birth to the modern-day organization, arrived in the 1920s, when the professional managers Pierre du Pont and Alfred Sloan structured their organizations into large command-and-control hierarchies—structures that existed for most of the twentieth century and still exist in many organizations to this day.

The third phase, asserted Drucker, marked "the shift from the command-and-control organization, the organization of departments and divisions, to the information-based organization of knowledge specialists."

Drucker added, "We can perceive, though perhaps only dimly, what this organization will look like. We can identify some of its main characteristics and requirements. But we can point to central problems of values, structure, and behavior. But the job of actually building the information-based organization is still ahead of us—it is the managerial challenge of the future."

The New Information Revolutions

A decade after the *Harvard Business Review* article, Drucker advanced his thinking when he espoused his "four revolution" theory. In *Management Challenges for the 21st Century* (1999), he described a new information revolution that will significantly affect all organizations across the globe.

Drucker describes this new revolution with great clarity: it is not taking place in management information systems (MIS) or information technology (IT), and is not being led by the chief information officer (CIO). He called it "a revolution in CONCEPTS."

As he explains it, for fifty years information technology has "centered on *data*—their collection, storage, transmission, presentation. It has focused on the T in IT. The new information revolutions focus on the I."

Today's revolutions are changing the manager's outlook. Today's managers are asking for more than data. They are demanding information that can help them make better decisions. Instead of mindlessly wading through their in-boxes (electronic or otherwise) or perusing the latest accounting report, they are now questioning the data. "What is report X for, or what is the meaning of report Y?" As a result, the revolutions are "redefining" what information is provided and changing the jobs of people who produce the information.

Drucker asserted, correctly, that he was one of a very few who foresaw the impact that the computer would have on the business world. But he also predicted that the computer would have its greatest impact on top management and its decision making. On that score, Drucker says he could not have been more wrong. Instead, the computer's greatest application has been on *operations.*

As examples he cites software that enables architects to design the intricate "innards" of big buildings in a day, or the software that permits surgeons to perform virtual operations. "Half a century ago," he explains, "no one could have imagined the software that enables a major equipment maker such as Caterpillar to organize its operations, including manufacturing worldwide, around the anticipated service and replacement needs of its customers."

However, despite the stunning advances, Drucker's stance did not change. He continued to assert that information technology has had little impact on helping managers decide *whether or not* to build a new office building or school or hospital, or *what to do* with the new office or school or hospital.

Similarly, computers have had little effect on helping

managers decide which markets to enter or exit, or which companies to acquire: "For top management tasks," Drucker explains, "information technology so far has been a producer of data rather than a producer of information—let alone a producer of new and different questions and new and different strategies."

The reason senior managers have not been enabled by the new technology has more to do with inertia than anything else. Since the early nineteenth century, organizations have been built on the assumption that a lower cost structure was one of the keys to helping companies better compete. The reports that companies have produced—ever since there have been large companies—have more to do with "the preservation of assets and for the distribution if the venture was liquidated."

However, by around World War II it dawned on thinkers like Drucker that preserving assets and controlling costs are not the first concerns of top management. These are operational tasks.

This does not mean that a huge cost disadvantage could not sink a business. But success in business is not based on controlling costs, but on "the creation of value and wealth," says Drucker.

Organizations create wealth by taking risks, by developing new strategies, and by abandoning yesterday. But none of the current accounting systems help senior managers make these critical decisions. "Top management's frustration with the data that information technology has provided has triggered the new, the next Information Revolution." That's why a new information model, which has ignited what Drucker calls the Fourth Information Revolution, is needed.

Drucker asserted that what was needed was "to define information," to make it more pertinent and actionable to the users of that information. Since 90 percent of the reports generated by organizations are still used to describe what goes on *inside* an organization, it is no wonder management's patience was running out. In recent years many senior managers figured out that they needed different kinds of reports and data in order to do their jobs better, and they began to demand them from their accounting and finance people. Drucker said this process began when top managers asked: "What information concepts do we need for our tasks?"

In discussing the four information revolutions, Drucker remained remarkably consistent in his belief that the last frontier of information has remained unexplored: "The new area ... and the most important one, in which we do not as yet have systematic and organized methods for obtaining information: information on the OUTSIDE of the enterprise. These new methods are very different in their assumptions and their origins. . . . They aim at providing information rather than data. And they are designed for top management and to provide information for top management tasks and top management decisions."

Drucker saw the information as something that would transcend business. "The new Information Revolution began in

business and has gone furthest in it. But it is about to revolu-
tionize education and health care. Again, the changes in concepts will be in the end at least as important as the changes in
tools and technology.... It is generally accepted now that education technology is due for profound changes and that with them
will come profound changes in structure. Long-distance learning, for instance, may well make obsolete within twenty-five
years that uniquely American institution, the freestanding un-
dergraduate college.

"In health care a similar conceptual shift is likely to lead
from health care being defined as the fight against disease to
being defined as the maintenance of physical and mental func-
tioning.... Neither of the traditional health care providers, the
hospital and the general practice physician, may survive this
change, and certainly not in their present form or function."

Drucker concluded that in both education and in health
care, the biggest shift will be from business data to information, from the T in IT to the I. Here are a few lessons gleaned
from Drucker's detailed discussion on the changing role of information in a business environment:

- **Information is most actionable when it tells
  you something about the outside: customers,
  noncustomers, and the marketplace.**
  Otherwise it is simply data. Understand that getting this
  type of information will be demand driven, once manag-

ers understand what they need to enhance productivity to better compete.

- **Help colleagues (for example, accountants and MIS people) understand the importance of obtaining information on the outside.**
  Then work with them to figure out exactly what you need to innovate to develop the breadwinners of tomorrow.

- **Don't wait for accountants or MIS.**
  The kind of change that Drucker is talking about—shifting to developing outside information—can take years. Be proactive in getting the information you need. Spend two to four hours per week on competitors' Web sites, in the marketplace, talking to customers, and doing anything else that will tell you more about what goes on outside the walls of your own organization.

The Electronic Revolution and the Power of Print

Drucker wrote of these information revolutions in the late 1990s, after the Internet had already begun to transform many industries. But once again, it was Drucker who saw through the obvious and the hype of the so-called New Economy, which was being touted in books and articles as a new utopia where the old rules of business no longer counted.

While many felt that the Internet would usurp the printed book, Drucker understood that the Internet strengthened the print media. He described how in *Management Challenges for the 21st Century*: "And now the printed media are taking over the electronic channels," he wrote. He noted that Amazon.com, "in a very few short years," has become the largest retailer on the Internet.

And it hasn't been only books that benefited from the Internet: "More and more of the specialty mass magazines," argued Drucker, "now publish an on-line edition—delivered over the Internet to be printed out by the subscriber. Instead of IT replacing print, print is taking over the electronic technology as a distribution channel for PRINTED INFORMATION."

However, it is not as simple as that. "The new distribution channel will surely change the printed book. New distribution channels always do change what they distribute. But however delivered or stored, it will remain a printed product. And it will still provide information," Drucker asserted.

"Beyond the Information Revolution"

In 1999, Drucker wrote another piece that advanced his thinking on the topic. Titled "Beyond the Information Revolution," it first appeared in *The Atlantic Monthly* and then in one of Drucker's final books, *Managing in the Next Society*. In this piece he provided additional insights on the information revolution when he discussed the advent of e-commerce and its place and impact on the information revolution. Here he examines yet another aspect of the information revolution:

"The truly revolutionary impact of the Information Revolution is just beginning to be felt. But it is not 'information' that fuels this impact. It is not 'artificial intelligence.' It is not the effect of computers . . . on decision-making policymaking, or strategy. It is something that practically no one foresaw, or even talked about ten or fifteen years ago—that is, the explosive emergence of the Internet as a major, perhaps eventually the major, worldwide distribution channel for goods, for services, and, surprisingly, for managerial and professional jobs. This is profoundly changing economies, markets and industry structures; products and services and their flows; consumer segmentation, consumer values, and consumer behavior; jobs and labor markets. But the impact may be even greater on societies and politics, and, above all, on the way we see the world and ourselves in it."

In this piece it became clear that Drucker not only believed in how and what information technology can do to transform an organization or a market, but he was also an avid believer and excited by the possibilities.

Explained Drucker, "At the same time, new and unexpected industries will no doubt emerge, and fast." He named biotechnology as one example. "It is likely that other new technologies will appear suddenly, leading to major new industries. What they may be it is impossible to even guess at. But it is highly probable—indeed, nearly certain—that they will emerge, and fairly fast. And it is nearly certain that few of them—and few industries based on them—will come out of computer and information technology.

"Of course, these are only predictions," Drucker continued. "But they are made on the assumption that the Information Revolution will evolve as several earlier technology-based 'revolutions' have evolved over the past five hundred years, since Gutenberg's printing revolution.... In particular the assumption is that the Information Revolution will be like the Industrial Revolution of the late eighteenth and early nineteenth centuries.

"The Information Revolution is now at the point at which the Industrial Revolution was in the early 1820s, about forty years after James Watt's improved steam engine.... The early industries of the Industrial Revolution—cotton, textiles, iron, the railroads—were boom industries that created millionaires overnight...the industries that emerged after 1830 also created millionaires. But they took twenty years to do so, and it was twenty years of hard work, of struggle, of disappointments and failures.... This is likely to be true of the industries that will emerge from now on. It is already true of biotechnology," contended Drucker.

Last, Drucker focused on the importance of attracting and holding on to the best people as perhaps the single most important determinant of success to the organizations of the future. And he felt strongly that money was not the answer: "Bribing the knowledge workers on whom these industries depend will therefore simply not work. . . . Increasingly, performance in these new knowledge-based industries will come to depend on running the institution so as to attract, hold, and motivate knowledge workers. When this can no longer be done by satisfying knowledge workers' greed, as we are now trying to do, it will have to be done by satisfying their values, and by giving them social recognition and social power. It will have to be done by turning them from subordinates into fellow executives, and from employees, however well paid, into partners."

The Fourth Information Revolution

Drucker's evolving views on information and his self-proclaimed information revolutions tell us a good deal about Drucker. At first he saw information as an internal tool to measure performance, but over the years he felt it increasingly important to use information as a tool to help managers better understand the outside (for example, customers, competitors, markets). However, as late as the closing years of the 1990s, Ducker was disappointed that 90 percent of the information produced by organizations was still looking inward. The greatest impetus for change will come from increasingly frustrated senior managers seeking more actionable information on customers, noncustomers, and markets.

However, Drucker saw information in several dimensions simultaneously. He was one of the first to recognize that computers would have great impact on business, but he also saw its limitations. Machines were "mechanical morons," and would never substitute for managers who make the tough decisions.

He also saw information revolutions as milestones in history, ones that separated one era from the next. The Fourth Information Revolution is not unprecedented, but it will usher in new industries. We cannot conceptualize what those industries will be, and it could take twenty years of hard work and struggle before things shake out. Ultimately, Drucker comes back to his key of valuing people over technology. Tomorrow's winning organizations will be those that attract and keep top people, not with stock options and other financial incentives but by turning them from subordinates into partners.

Chapter 14

The Leader's Most Important Job

"One has to make the organization capable of anticipating the storm, weathering it, and in fact, being ahead of it."

In many of his works, Drucker made it abundantly clear that all managers must be ready to deal proactively with impending disasters. "Leadership is a foul-weather job," proclaimed Drucker in 1990. As he explained to me: "Hospitals love crises," but crises are not restricted to hospital emergency rooms. All leaders must be prepared to deal with crises. "The most important task of an organization's leader is to anticipate crisis. Perhaps not to avert it, but to anticipate it. To wait until the crisis hits is already abdication," he said.

During our lunch, Drucker steered our conversation to one of his favorite topics: nonprofit organizations. It was not something I expected to cover with him, since I had never envisioned writing a book for nonprofit managers. Frankly, I had always regarded nonprofits as "softer" to run than an operating unit or company with P&L responsibility. But two things quickly became clear: one, this was a subject that inspired Drucker, and two, many of the key lessons that applied to nonprofits also applied to managers of for-profit companies.

As discussed in chapter 3, he started working with nonprofits as early as the 1950s. Over the years Drucker worked with such organizations as CARE, The Salvation Army, the American Red Cross, the Navajo Tribal Council, the American Heart Association, and his local Episcopal church in La Verne, California, often taking no fees for his work.

By the 1980s he felt that nonprofits needed him and his management wisdom even more than for-profit corporations, for two specific reasons. First, he told me, "Too many nonprofits, especially large ones ... have no clear sense of mission." But he felt the second problem was even more worrisome: "The central problem is that there is no such thing as a bottom line in a nonprofit. And while profit in a business is a very poor measurement, it's a discipline."

That's when I repeated back to Drucker one of his favorite tenets: "There are no profit centers within a company, only cost centers."

"It's worse than that," Drucker shot back. He said that in most nonprofits, especially local community nonprofits, when they don't get the desired results, they simply do more of the same. "So they don't abandon anything. They put their best people on it, where they have no results." "They put their best people where they have no results" is yet another Druckerism, and an important concept for corporations and nonprofits alike.

A Foul-Weather Job

While Drucker felt that nonprofits had their own issues to deal with, he also understood before anyone else that nonprofits needed to be managed. He explained that TV and newspaper people who interviewed him assumed that the only reason nonprofits hired him was to help in fund-raising. Drucker refuted that: "We work together on their mission, their leadership, their management." The reporter would shoot back, "That's *business* management, isn't it?" These journalists were skeptical, implying that nonprofits were one-dimensional enterprises that needed nothing more than cash infusions to survive.

Drucker set them straight. He argued that "the non-profit institutions need management all the more because they do not have a conventional 'bottom line.' They know they need to learn how to use management as their tool lest they be overwhelmed by it. They know they need management so that they can concentrate on their mission."

It was this thinking that led Drucker to write the book *Managing the Non-Profit Organization* (1990),* a book that was passed

---

* This book started out as a series of twenty-one one-hour audio cassettes entitled *Leadership and Management in the Non-Profit Institution* (also known as *The Non-Profit Drucker*).

over by most company executives for obvious reasons. However, in overlooking the book, managers missed out on one of Drucker's compelling writings on leadership, the chapter titled "Leadership is a Foul-Weather Job." Many of the excerpts in this chapter are from that oft-overlooked book.

If the Market Grows, Grow with It

Ironically, one of the other causes of crisis is success. "Problems of success have ruined more organizations than has failure, partly because if things go wrong, everybody knows they have to go to work," wrote Drucker. "Success creates its own euphoria. You outrun your resources. And you retire on the job, which may be the most difficult thing to fight."

Drucker used his own career as a prime example. He left New York University after twenty years because NYU's graduate school of business (today the Stern School of Business) decided to cut back rather than expand to meet the increasing demands of a quickly growing student population. The university created its own crisis in making the decision not to grow, even when market conditions indicated that to be a poor move.

When Drucker went to Claremont, California, to build a management school, he made sure to do it right. "I made sure that we did not overextend ourselves. I was very careful to ensure that we kept the faculty first rate but small, and that we used adjuncts, part-time people, [and] then built a strong administration. And then we can run with success. If the market grows, you have to grow with it, or you become marginal."

The Key Competencies

For an organization to be successful—and *stay* successful—its senior management team must be capable of staying one step ahead of an impending storm. That is called "innovation, constant renewal," in Drucker's lexicon.

"You cannot prevent a major catastrophe," he declared, "but you can build an organization that is battle-ready, that has high morale, and also has been through a crisis, knows how to behave, trusts itself, and where people trust one another. In military training, the first rule is to instill soldiers with trust in their officers, because without trust they won't fight."

Drucker also described the opposite type of leader. He said not everyone is afraid of crises: "[Some] people are beautifully prepared for the crises. And hate everything else."

As a vivid example of someone who thrived under intense pressure, Drucker turned to Winston Churchill. Drucker called Churchill the twentieth century's most successful leader. However, for a dozen years, from 1928 through Dunkirk (where more than three hundred thousand allied soldiers were successfully evacuated), Churchill was at best an onlooker, "almost discredited," claimed Drucker, "because there was no need for a Churchill."

When disaster struck and England was forced to declare war on Germany in 1939, Churchill emerged as an important, decisive figure on the world stage and exactly what the country needed at the time. (The admiration was not all one-sided: Winston Churchill once said, "The amazing thing about Peter F. Drucker was his ability to start our minds along a stimulating line of thought."*)

Drucker asserted: "Fortunately or unfortunately, the one thing in any organization is the crisis. That always comes. That's when you *do* depend on the leader."

Drucker felt that leaders like Churchill were rare indeed. "But another group is, fortunately, quite common," wrote Drucker. "They are the people who can look at a situation and say: This is not what I was hired to do or what I expected to do, but this is what the job requires—and then roll up their sleeves and go to work."

"To every leader there is a season. There is a profundity in that statement, but it's not quite that simple," wrote Drucker. "Winston Churchill in ordinary, peaceful, normal times would not have been very effective. He needed the challenge. Probably the same is true of Franklin D. Roosevelt, who was basically a lazy man," contended Drucker. "I don't think FDR would have been a good president in the 1920s. His adrenaline wouldn't have produced.

---

* Churchill praised Drucker's first book, *The End of Economic Man*, in *The Times Literary Supplement*, May 27, 1939.

"On the other hand, there are people who are very good when things are pretty routine, but who can't take the stress of an emergency. Most organizations need somebody who can lead regardless of the circumstances. What matters is that he works on the basic competences," Drucker declared. Drucker had definite ideas on what it took to lead in good times and bad, and spelled out those competences:

- "The willingness, ability, and self-discipline to listen" topped Drucker's list as the most important competence for an "all-weather" leader.
  "Anybody can do it," he insisted. "All you have to do is keep your mouth shut."

- The next competence "is the willingness to communicate, to make yourself understood."
  "This requires infinite patience. We never outgrow age three in that respect," wrote Drucker honestly. "You have to tell us again and again and again. And demonstrate what you mean."

- The third competence "is not to alibi yourself."
  Drucker felt that foul-weather leaders take responsibility for what doesn't work, and insist on a standard of excellence: "We either do things to perfection or we don't do them."

● **The last competence is an "understanding of how unimportant you are when compared to the task."**
Leaders need a certain detachment, felt Drucker. "They subordinate themselves to the task, but don't identify themselves with the task. The task remains both bigger than they are, and different." Drucker said the greatest indictment of a leader is that the organization falls apart the day he or she leaves. "He or she hasn't built. They may have been effective operators, but they have not created vision," wrote Drucker. Leaders must learn to become servants to whatever task the organization needs to perform.

Drucker felt that pettiness and ego were the enemy of effective leadership, and once again he referred to Churchill and FDR to draw a contrast between two types of leaders. He felt that one of Churchill's greatest strengths was that he nurtured the careers of young politicians, even as an old man in his nineties (as did Drucker). "That is a hallmark of the truly effective leader, who doesn't feel threatened by strength. In his last years, FDR systematically cut down everybody who showed any signs of independence," wrote Drucker. That was a most controversial statement for Drucker; after all, FDR was one of the twentieth century's most beloved American presidents and a leader who possessed certain key strengths.

Self-made Leaders

When writing of "foul-weather" leaders, Drucker contrasted born leaders with those who acquired their skills along the way. "Most leaders I've seen were neither born nor made. They were self-made. We need far too many leaders to depend only on the naturals." One of Drucker's favorite examples of a leader who was not a natural, not trained, but developed into an effective leader, was President Harry Truman.

"When Truman became president, he was totally unprepared," claimed Drucker, who also asserted that Truman was selected by FDR because Roosevelt felt he posed no threat. Drucker was impressed with Truman's "the buck stops here" philosophy. But more important, even though he had no foreign policy experience, he quickly grasped the fact that his focus had to be beyond U.S. borders, on international affairs. He asked that all-so-critical Drucker question, "What needs to be done?"

"He forced himself to take a crash course in foreign affairs and to focus—painfully—on what he considered to be new tasks."

Truman wasn't the only leader Drucker respected. Although he regarded General Douglas MacArthur as terribly vain, he thought him one of the last great strategists and a "brilliant man." But it was neither his intelligence nor his strategic mind that was his great strength. "He [MacArthur] built a team second to none because he put the task first," argued Drucker. One of his secrets was that he ran meetings in a way that ran counter to every fiber in his being.

Despite his huge ego, MacArthur was disciplined enough to listen to the most junior officer first in every staff meeting. This was a gut-wrenching, counterintuitive exercise for the general, but he made sure to do it because he knew that the success of his unit depended on it. Drucker felt it was one of the keys to helping MacArthur fight and win against forces far more formidable than his own.

Balance Is the Key

Drucker felt that one of the great challenges for leaders was striking the balance between being too cautious and being too impulsive. Drucker said that he was one of those who always expected results too soon. To counter that, he lessened his expectations: "I taught myself that if I expect something to happen in three months, I say, make it five. But I've also seen people who say three years when they should say three months. As in all Aristotelian means, the first law is 'Know thyself.' Know your degenerative tendency."

Drucker witnessed more companies hurt by cautiousness and indecision than rashness and risk-taking. "Maybe I'm conscious of it because I was over-cautious when I ran institutions, or was part of the running. I did not take risks, especially financial risks I should have taken," said Drucker.

He also contended that there had to be a "balanced decision

between opportunity and risk. One asks first: is the decision reversible? If it is, one usually can take considerable risks. Then," explained Drucker, "one asks is it a risk we can afford?" The manager should obviously not take any risk that can kill the company. A little pain is tolerable, but the company's future should not be compromised by one decision that goes bad.

One of the most difficult situations for managers was saying yes to something that carried great risk but was too good to pass up. Drucker described a personal anecdote to explain this situation. He had once sat on a museum board in which a huge, expensive collection was up for sale, at a price tag beyond what the museum could afford. Nonetheless, the museum was offered a chance to buy it. When members of the board asked Drucker what they should do, he said, "Damn the torpedoes, let's buy it. It's the last chance we'll have. It will make us a first-class museum. We'll get the money somehow."

When I reread *Managing the Non-Profit Organization* after I interviewed Drucker, I was struck by two things. First, this book was one of the rare Drucker books in which he opened up and shared personal stories and anecdotes, with the exception of his autobiography, which he said was not an autobiography. (See the Epilogue for some clarification of this comment.)

The other thing that struck me was that despite his tendency for self-deprecation, he was more of a manager than he let on. He told me that he had never *managed* anything, that he knew nothing about management "from the inside." But he had a hand in building and running the then Peter F. Drucker Graduate School of Management at Claremont Graduate University. He also helped make countless decisions for hundreds of companies and nonprofits over the years. When he confessed to being "the world's worst manager" who had "no experience," he was stretching, to say the least. As a teacher, consultant, and mentor, he played a key role in more decisions than do most CEOs in a lifetime.

The Leader's Most Important Job

One of the biggest mistakes both nonprofits and corporations make is that they "put their best people where they have no results." That error can cause a crisis if left unchecked. It sounds like an obvious problem, but human resources are easily misallocated. To make sure you don't make the same mistake, make a list of your key people and the results they have achieved in the last year. Do you have the best people assigned where they can make the greatest contribution, where the best opportunities are? Or are resources being wasted, as your best people put out fires?

No matter how effective the leader, crisis will eventually come to every organization. That's when the leader must step up. This will often entail actions that transcend job descriptions, but when crisis comes, one does not look at memos or reports. Instead, one acts. This entails four specific competencies: the self-discipline to listen, the willingness to communicate often and make sure you are understood, the willingness to take responsibility and not "alibi yourself," and the willingness to place the organization's goals above your own.

The strongest leaders, insisted Drucker, do not fear strength, they encourage it. Last, they are balanced in their decision making. They take calculated risks, but they don't make a habit of betting the company's entire future. The one exception is the risk that a company cannot afford to miss, as in Drucker's "damn the torpedoes" museum example.

Chapter 15

A Short Course on Innovation

"Businesses prefer not to abandon the old, the obsolescent, the no-longer-productive; they'd rather hang on to it and keep on pouring money into it. Worse still, they then assign their most capable people to "defending" the outworn in a massive misallocation of the scarcest and most valuable resource—the human resource that needs to be allocated to making tomorrow, if the company is to have a tomorrow."

Peter Drucker was the first management writer to talk and write about innovation as a key management practice. In the preface of his 1985 book devoted to the topic, *Innovation and Entrepreneurship*, Drucker commented that it was only in the last few years—meaning the early 1980s—that business authors began to "pay much attention to innovation and entrepreneurship." He pointed out that his 1985 book was "the first work that attempts to present the subject in its entirety and in systematic form."

By the time that book was published, Drucker had been writing, consulting, or teaching about innovation for thirty years. But he told me that he could not have written a convincing book totally devoted to the topic until he was ready. Drucker told me that his consulting was his "laboratory," but what complicated matters was that all of his consulting assignments were different. Since no two organizations were alike, it made it difficult to draw conclusions that would apply to all corporations. "Writing is merely the last stage," he explained. "By the time I wrote it, I must have understood it, and practiced it for some time."

Drucker then provided some additional background. He explained that he had taught his first course in innovation in 1958 or so, and out of that seminar half a dozen major businesses had grown. The most well-known company to come out of the session was Donaldson, Lufkin & Jenrette, the investment bank founded in 1959. Another manager who attended that seminar was the circulation manager of the "dying" *Saturday Evening Post*, who later founded *Psychology Today*. However, Drucker waited more than twenty-five years to write a book on the topic because he had not done enough "to feel really confident on the topic." He had not tested it.

It is no accident that this chapter follows the chapter on managing crisis. Drucker saw innovation as the key to averting crisis and keeping companies strong; he saw complacency and insularity as the enemies of innovation. That was clear in all of his management books since *The Practice of Management*.

This chapter will also include a discussion of how two modern-day authors, one a practitioner, Andy Grove, and the second, a well-known professor and consultant, Clay Christensen, have made significant contributions to the field of innovation by building, in one way or another, on the body of knowledge Drucker established in the 1950s.

Making the Future Happen

No book that purports to get inside Drucker's mind could fulfill its objective without acknowledging his contribution to the topic of innovation. So much of his work is devoted to getting managers to see things as they are, how they *could* be, and how they *should* be. He viewed purposeful abandonment as a precursor to innovation, for unless an organization abandoned products "before they really want to," a genuine innovation couldn't take hold.

In Drucker's view, many managers get too bogged down in the day-to-day operations of the company: "Tomorrow always arrives," he wrote. "It is always different. And then even the mightiest company is in trouble if it has not worked on the future. It will have lost distinction and leadership—all that will remain is big-company overhead.... Not having dared to take the risk of making the new happen, it perforce took the much greater risk of being surprised by what did happen.... And this is a risk that even the largest and richest company cannot afford and that even the smallest business need not run.

"The executive has to accept responsibility for making the future happen," continued Drucker. "It is the willingness to tackle purposefully this, the last of the economic tasks in business enterprise that distinguishes the great business from the merely competent one, and the business builder from the executive-suite custodian."

What Will Our Business Be?

Drucker first wrote his doctrine about business purpose and the primacy of the customer in *The Practice of Management* in the mid-1950s: "The customer is the foundation of the business and keeps it in existence.

"Because its purpose is to create a customer," continued Drucker, "any business enterprise has two—and only these two—basic functions: marketing and innovation. They are the entrepreneurial functions. . . . A business is set apart from all other human organizations by the fact that it markets a product or a service.

"The second function of a business is therefore innovation," he added. "It is not enough for the business to provide just any economic goods and services; it must provide better and more economic ones. It is not necessary for a business to grow bigger; but it is necessary that it constantly grow better."

Drucker added that a lower price can represent an innovation. "But it may also be a new and better product (even at a higher price), a new convenience or the creation of a new want. It may be finding new uses for old products."

Even at this early stage in Drucker's career, he viewed innovation as something that must become part of an organization's DNA, and not as a distinct activity that gets assigned to one or more executives: "Innovation goes right through all phases of business ... innovation extends through all forms of business," he wrote. "In the organization of business enterprise innovation can therefore no more be considered a separate function than marketing.

"Indeed, what the customer considers value is so complicated that it can only be answered by the customer himself. Management should not even try to guess at it—it should always go to the customer in a systematic quest for the answer."

Drucker argued that management must also ask, "What will our business be?" Answering that question depended on these four things:

- **What is the market potential and market trend?** Management must make a prediction about the size of the market five or ten years down the line, "assuming no basic changes in market structure and technology." Also, a manager must be able to make a calculation on precisely what factors will shape the markets in the future.

- Second, "**What changes in market structure** are to be expected as the result of economic developments, changes in fashion or taste, or moves by the competition?" And by "competition" Drucker reminded managers that competitors must be defined by the customer's perception (in other words, it must be viewed outside-in, not inside out).

- Next, "What innovations will change the customer's wants, create new ones, extinguish old ones, create new ways of satisfying his wants, change his concept of value or make it possible to give him greater value satisfaction?"

- Last, "What wants does the consumer have that are not being adequately satisfied by the products or services offered him today?" This is a critical question facing every company. Drucker insisted that those organizations that can get this answer right are likely to achieve healthy growth. Those that can't will be at the mercy of outside factors and circumstances, such as the "rising tide of its economy or industry. And whoever contents himself to rise with the tide will also fall with it."

Too many organizations have a hard time figuring out what to grow and what to abandon, as Drucker explained in 1982: "A growth policy needs to be able to distinguish between healthy growth, fat, and cancer—all three are 'growth,' but surely all three are not equally desirable. . . . A lot of growth in an inflationary period is pure fat. But some of it is also precancerous."

Drucker was telling managers to exercise careful judgment by abandoning the marginal. "Yesterday's breadwinner should almost always be abandoned on a fairly fast schedule," explains Drucker. "It still may produce net revenue. But it soon becomes a bar to the introduction and success of tomorrow's breadwinner."

Only with new ideas and purposeful innovation can a company stay ahead of the pack, and anytime an organization is behind the curve is a perilous time. That's why Drucker argued so forcefully for organizations to abandon the "old," even when it appeared that the "old" was still going strong. But it takes great discipline to let go of products or other offerings when they *appear* to be healthy, or at least pulling their weight by covering their costs.

Organize for Innovation

Every organization seeking growth must organize itself to "look for innovation," asserted Drucker in 1990. "The starting point," insisted Drucker, "is to recognize that change is not a threat, but an opportunity." The key is to identify those changes that signify a genuine opportunity, such as unanticipated success in your organization.

To make his point, Drucker cited two examples: the first detailed the explosion in continuing education in the United States in the 1980s. He said that this was not a "luxury" or "something to bring in additional money or good public relations. It is becoming the central thrust of our knowledge society."

The second example of change that could help managers seize on future opportunities is the diversification of population and demographics. In the late 1970s, the Girl Scouts of the USA understood that the increasing diversity of the population offered a new opportunity for the organization, and they took advantage of it and grew accordingly.

"The lesson is, don't wait," implored Drucker. "Organize yourself for systematic innovation. Build the search for opportunities, inside and outside, into your organization. Look for changes as indications of an opportunity for innovation."

To make sure that innovation is given top priority, reasoned Drucker, the leader must set the example. The challenge is to establish and foster a culture that encourages innovative decision making throughout the ranks, but at the same time permits the company to go on operating at 100 percent while the changes are taking place. Drucker outlined several steps to make this happen.

"First, organize yourself to see the opportunity. If you don't look out the window you won't see it." This is critical because most of the reports that are generated by the IT or accounting departments only report on the past, on what has already happened. They reveal problem areas, they don't pinpoint opportunities. "So we have to go beyond our reporting systems," said Drucker. "And whenever you need a change, ask: If this is an opportunity for us, what would it be?"

To make sure that innovation takes hold, there are a few other steps that managers must take. Drucker explained that the number one killer of innovation is an organization that tries to hedge its bets, that is, a company that tries to have it both ways. It talks a good game of innovation but doesn't fully commit. Instead it holds on too tight to the past.

The next challenge is "operating the new." Any new venture needs to be given enough room to succeed. This means that it must be organized as a separate unit. "Babies don't belong in the living room, they belong in the nursery," insisted Drucker. "It is far too perilous to put the new concepts, the new ideas, into operating units, regardless of what it is. That's because the solving of the daily crisis will always take precedence over introducing tomorrow. So, when you try to develop the new within an existing operation, you are always postponing tomorrow. It must be set up separately. And yet you have to make sure the existing operations don't lose the excitement of the new entirely. Otherwise, they become not only hostile but paralyzed."

Innovation Down the Barrel of a Gun

In some situations, companies innovate because they have no choice. Sometimes something happens—something so dramatic in the market, with a competitor or some other political event—that forces management's hand. When that happens, an organization must innovate or perish.

One classic example is Sam Walton and the founding of Wal-Mart. In 1962, roughly the same year that Target and Kmart were founded, Sam Walton opened his first Wal-Mart. At the time, Sam Walton had more than a dozen stores, but none of them were discount stores. Discounting was already a $2 billion industry, and Walton feared that if he did not change his retailing model, he would be steamrolled by the innovation in retailing that was sweeping across America. Walton's hand was forced by a new breed of competitor. The rest is history. Walton's model of discounting, honed by years of studying competitors and seeking continual improvement, crushed competitors and made Wal-Mart a true "category killer." The company would, of course, emerge as the word's largest retailer.

Andy Grove, the cofounder and former CEO of Intel, knows a great deal about this kind of change—change that is powerful enough to force a company's executives to rethink their entire strategy. He described this phenomenon in his book *Only the Paranoid Survive* (1996).

Intel had been the industry's dominant manufacturer of memory chips for more than a decade. Because of its first-mover advantage, Intel had nearly 100 percent of the memory chip market. That was about to change, and in stunning fashion.

By the mid-1980s the Japanese had found a way to break Intel's hold on the market. Not only were the chips coming from Japanese rivals superior in quality, they were also cheaper. Grove felt that Intel had contributed to its own problems by being late to market with some key new products and had moved too slowly in building new factories.*

Once the Japanese had gained the upper hand in the memory chip market, Intel's fate was sealed. No matter how the firm tried to regain its advantage, it failed. Grove later described that dire situation: "You execute on the wrong strategy, you sink. You don't execute on the right strategy, you sink.... Our execution, and our strategy, were faulty."

The unfortunate reality is that the situation was so bad that the company was left with no good options. "The need for a different memory strategy, one that would stop the hemorrhage, was growing urgent," insisted Grove.

If Intel did the unthinkable by exiting the memory chip market, they would be abandoning the cash cow that had built the company. But they had no choice. As Grove explained it, they "had become marginalized by our Japanese competitors. There really was no viable option for us to work our way out.... The defining business of the company had not hit a pothole but an ultimate wall, and we had to make a very desperate move."

That's when he and his cofounder made the fateful decision to get out of the memory business. They were forced to eliminate about one third of the company over a very painful three-year period. However, there was a light at the end of the tunnel.

---

* A version of this story was included in my 2003 book, *What the Best CEOs Know* (McGraw-Hill).

The company decided to focus on microprocessors. Although it wasn't a big part of their business, Intel had been supplying microprocessors to IBM for its PCs for five years. In addition, microprocessors were the future. Memory chips were limited to storing memory, while microprocessors could actually perform calculations. They were the thinking part of the computer. After a very painful few years, Intel would become the leading maker of microprocessors in the industry.

Unfortunately for Grove and Intel, in this situation they were reactive, not proactive. They changed only when they had to, precisely the situation Drucker warned against when he said, "Even the mightiest company is in trouble if it has not worked on the future." Intel had not "dared to take the risk of making the new happen."

The chief goal of Grove's book *Only the Paranoid Survive* was to warn managers of this kind of seismic change—what he called "a strategic inflection point"—or "a ten times force" (meaning ten times as powerful as anything that had come before it). That degree of change has the potential to put an organization out of business—permanently. Grove characterized a strategic inflection point as "a time in the life of a business in which its fundamentals are about to change."

Grove later added that strategic inflection points "represent, in my description of it, what happens to a business when a major change takes place in its competitive environment." Grove observed that strategic inflection points are not restricted to changes in technology. Many things can lead to one, including a change in regulations, new or shifting competition, or a new channel of distribution.

His personal example of Intel's battle with the Japanese is a prime example of a strategic inflection point. So is the world of retailing that Sam Walton was up against in the early 1960s, when discounting was just beginning to become an industry phenomenon. The biggest difference in these two cases is that Walton got ahead of the change. Before altering his business model, Walton visited the leaders of these discounting businesses, asked countless questions, visited competitors' stores, and learned as much as he could. In Drucker's parlance, he changed "before he had to," since discounting was still years away from becoming the dominant form of retailing (and ironically, it would be Walton's Wal-Mart that would put more stores out of business than any retailer before or since).

One sure sign of a strategic inflection point is that "what used to work no longer works." In his case, Grove had admitted, "We had lost our bearings. We were wandering in the "valley of death"—defined by Grove as "the perilous transition between the old and the new ways of doing business." He added, "You march in knowing full well that some of your colleagues will not make it across to the other side. Yet the senior manager's task is to force that march to a vaguely perceived goal in spite of the casualties, and the middle manager's responsibility is to support that decision. There is no other choice."

Andy Grove quoted Peter Drucker several times in *Only the*

Paranoid Survive, and later acknowledged Drucker's contributions to his own thinking. "Like many philosophers," Grove wrote of Drucker, "he spoke in plain language that resonated with ordinary managers. Consequently, simple statements from him have influenced untold numbers of daily actions; they did mine over decades."

Grove cited Drucker when he explained that the key activity required in the course of transforming an organization—getting through the "valley of death"—"is a wholesale shifting of resources from what was appropriate for the old idea of the business to what is appropriate for the new." "To make it through the valley of death successfully," explained Grove, "your first task is to form a mental image of what the company should look like when you get to the other side."

Grove explained that over the next three years his production planners shifted company resources from memory chips to microprocessors. "They were shifting rare and valuable resources from an area of lower value to an area of higher value." Grove pointed out that that was how Drucker defined entrepreneurship: moving resources from areas of lower productivity into areas of higher productivity and greater yield.*

Grove and Drucker agreed that it isn't only physical resources that must be redeployed, but human ones as well: "The

---

* Drucker credited French economist J. B. Say circa 1800, in the book *Innovation and Entrepreneurship*, for the concept of shifting of resources from lower areas of productivity to higher-yield areas.

scarcest resources in any organization are *performing people*," concluded Drucker.

Strategic inflection points can strike most any company in any industry at any time. The online brokers, for example, such as TD AMERITRADE or E*TRADE, served up a strategic inflection point to traditional stock brokers like Merrill Lynch. Practically overnight, countless millions of dollars in commissions disappeared as investors had the power to buy a thousand shares of a stock for the same commission as a New York City movie ticket.

Grove offered several suggestions in *Only the Paranoid Survive* to help companies either anticipate a strategic inflection point or diminish its impact. One important way was to listen to "helpful Cassandras," those paranoid types who constantly fear that the sky is falling and the end is near. Grove felt it was these extreme types—who are usually out in the field and more likely to have an outside-in perspective—who have the best chance of detecting a sea change before it turns into a full-fledged strategic inflection point. "They usually know more about upcoming change than the senior management because they spend so much time 'outdoors' where the winds of the real world blow in their faces," insisted Grove. They are often in middle management and often in sales. And you don't have to worry about finding them. They will seek you out, asserted Grove, and pass their fears directly to management.

Grove also advised managers to experiment often and "let chaos reign." Unless organizations experiment constantly with new ideas, concepts, processes, and products, it will be too late to counter the incredible punch of a strategic inflection point once one shows up at the firm's doorstep.

That line of thought mirrored Drucker's—he had been writing about a closely related topic, purposeful abandonment, for decades.

Drucker felt that managers, as a rule, did not do enough of what Andy Grove advocated. Most CEOs are too insulated, too cut off from the markets they serve. They spend too much time dealing with internal problems rather than searching for new opportunities.

CEOs did not ask the right questions often enough; nor did they spend enough time looking for *changes* in trends. Drucker felt that trend watching was insufficient—it was monitoring *shifts* in trends that made the difference and helped managers detect the kind of seismic changes that Grove described, the kind that could sink a company if left unchecked.

Disruptive Technologies

Peter Drucker and Andy Grove were not the only ones talking and writing about the forces that turn markets upside down. Harvard Business School's Clayton Christensen is the author of one of the most successful business books of the 1990s, and the most successful book on innovation ever published: *The Innovator's Dilemma*. (The hardcover edition was so successful that the book garnered a $1 million advance for the paperback rights, an almost unheard-of sum for a business book.) Although Grove was the practitioner and Christensen the academic (and consultant), both men held similar views of the world.

Christensen's *Innovator's Dilemma* concludes that the most successful companies are often the ones that get blindsided by a new or emerging technology. Clay Christensen called the new product that wreaks havoc on an established market a "disruptive technology." Andy Grove called it "the Christensen effect." *Forbes* magazine called it a "stealth attack."

A disruptive technology offers a new value proposition. It is "simpler and cheaper and lower performing," asserted Christensen. It is usually accompanied by lower margins and lower profits. Since few firms seek to develop new products with lower margins and lower profits, it is not surprising that it is often the largest mainstream companies that get taken by surprise when a disruptive technology comes along.

The primary purpose of Clay Christensen's *Innovator's Dilemma* was to figure out why many of the best-run companies falter. Christensen's research confirmed that a company's success is often the impetus for the missteps that follow: "They often fail," asserted Christensen, "because the very management practices that have allowed them to become industry leaders also make it extremely difficult for them to develop the disruptive technologies that ultimately steal away their markets."

Christensen's "disruptive technology" or "disruptive innovation" almost always refers to an innovation in technology that creates a new product or service that replaces the existing technology and changes the dynamics of a market. A strategic inflection point is a broader concept, since it can be brought on by nontechnological factors or events (think of what prohibition did to the liquor business).* However, both have the potential to derail a company overnight.

The following are examples of disruptive technologies and the sustaining technologies they challenged or replaced:

Established Technology	Disruptive Technology
Horse and buggy	Cars
Bricks and mortar bookstores	Online bookstores
Graduate schools of business	Corporate universities
Standard textbooks	Custom-made digital textbooks
Traditional 35-millimeter film photography	Digital photography
Multivolume, printed encyclopedia	Wikipedia (free online encyclopedia)

---

* In 2008, in his newsletter *Strategy & Innovation*, Christensen expanded his view of disruption when he asserted disruption is not limited to technology. Lower prices, working with different suppliers or different value chains can also cause a disruption.

In the closing pages of *Innovator's Dilemma*, Clay Christensen gives managers the following advice in his reader's guide: organizations should "give responsibility for disruptive technologies to organizations whose customers need them so that resources will flow to them."

He also felt it important that responsibility for a disruptive technology not be thrown into the mix with other more established mainstream products. Instead, he strongly recommended that a corporation should "set up a separate organization small enough to get excited by small gains." That precise recommendation was also made by Drucker, as discussed on page 216 of this chapter.

Third, Christensen told managers to "plan for failure." He urged executives not to bet everything "on being right the first time." Instead, he told managers to think of turning disruptive technologies into commercial products as "learning opportunities," and to course correct when necessary.

Last, "Don't count on breakthroughs." He instructed managers to move quickly and look for opportunities *outside* of the mainstream market. That's where the new market will be. The characteristics that make the new offering appealing to the smaller emerging market are the same ones that will make it unattractive to the mainstream market.

It was that kind of counterintuitive thinking that made *Innovator's Dilemma* such a compelling proposition that it was embraced by reviewers, practitioners, and academia.

Both Grove and Christensen were generous in their praise

of Peter Drucker. At an Academy of Management meeting in August of 1998, Grove spoke publicly of how he had been changed by reading Drucker's *Practice of Management* thirty years after it was written. Christensen called Drucker "an intellectual terrorist" for planting bombs that would go off in "unsuspecting readers' brains sometimes years later when triggered by a related event."

A Short Course in Innovation

Peter Drucker was the first business writer to attack the topic of innovation in systematic fashion. The key is to make sure to organize for innovation. "If you don't look out the window, you won't see it," urged Drucker, adding: "Tomorrow always arrives. It is always different. And then even the mightiest company is in trouble if it has not worked on the future. It will have lost distinction and leadership."

Andy Grove and Clay Christensen wrote of powerful forces that can turn markets upside down, thus forcing organizations to change or risk being made irrelevant. However, long before Grove's "strategic inflection point" and Christensen's "disruptive technology" became parts of the business lexicon, there was Peter Drucker, warning of similar perils but using less lofty terms.

Although his work was as groundbreaking as Grove's and Christensen's, he received little press attention for his findings. This is not surprising, since this was the plotline of

Drucker's career, the latter part in particular. By the 1990s, Drucker and his business books had been around for half a century, and even though his books continued to sell in strong numbers (tens of thousands compared to Grove's and Christensen's hundreds of thousands), many considered him old news.

In contrast, Grove and Christensen were new, even hip, which is why the press breathlessly announced their achievements. A prime example is a 1997 *Forbes* magazine cover featuring both Grove and Christensen (Christensen has a framed rendition of it hung in his office). In his later years—until just after his death in late 2005—one would be hard-pressed to find Drucker's face on the cover of a major business magazine like *Fortune* or *BusinessWeek*.

Epilogue

From the Monster to the Lamb: The People Who Shaped Peter Drucker

"But while my writings for fifty years have been stressing organic design, decentralization, and diversity, they deal with ideas, that is, with abstractions. I want executives to apply whatever I can teach. My aim has never been academic, that is, to be recognized; it has always been to make a difference."

This book has been more than five years in the making; however, I began to contemplate it long before then, ever since editing my first book on Jack Welch in the early 1990s.* It was then that I discovered the deep-rooted connection involving Welch, GE, and Drucker. I wanted to know more about this enigmatic man behind the shadowy curtain, who cooked up a discipline without ever managing anything on his

---

* That book was Robert Slater's *The New GE: How Jack Welch Revived an American Institution* (Homewood, IL: Dow Jones Irwin), published in the fall of 1991.

own. "Why was his work so influential?" was the first question that came to mind when I began to learn about what he had done at GE. I wanted to know what made this man tick, this self-described "writer" who had the ear of the most accomplished CEOs of the modern era.

After I interviewed Drucker, I spent a long time turning the recorded tapes into a printed transcript. Because of his very thick accent and hearing problem, transcribing those tapes took most of a year (working on them when time permitted). As a result, I got to "relive" that interview for many months as his words played over and over in my mind.

During those same months I read several of his books for the second or third time. The books were the same, but they took on a different meaning after our time together. He had a marvelous mind that was, for a writer, both asset and liability.

As I reread his works, I realized that while Drucker was an incredibly prolific writer, his books are not the easiest to read or navigate. His ideas, or concepts, as he called them, were usually better than the words he used to describe them. Even his most seminal works contain chapters or sections that are uneven and at times hard to follow.

He had a tendency for repetition, for digression, and for bringing in unfathomable ideas that at times distracted readers from his main thesis. It was as if his mind raced forward as he wrote and he had to work to keep up. He included all of his thoughts, often without an internal editor who might have kept his books on track. I often wondered how much help he got from the editors he worked with (I suspected that he maintained tight editorial control over each of his books, turning down the need for help even if offered); I also wondered what it would have been like to edit him.

The book I could not wait to read again was Drucker's favorite and most personal, *Adventures of a Bystander*, a book that is commonly referred to as his autobiography but is more like a memoir. As Drucker explains it, *Bystander* is a book he wrote for himself. The subtitle of the British version summed up Drucker's goal for the book: *Other Lives and My Times*. That is an accurate depiction of the book, which paints vivid portraits of the people who had the greatest impact on him.

"The book is no more a 'history of our times,' or even of '*my* times,' than it is an autobiography," he claimed in the prologue of the book. But it would have to do, for it was as close as Drucker would get to an actual autobiography. He was too humble to write a book that was chiefly about himself. He also maintained that he was not interesting enough to warrant a memoir.

"Bystanders have no history of their own," he wrote. "They are on stage but are not part of the action. They are not even audience. The fortunes of the play and of every actor on it depend on the audience whereas the reaction of the bystander has no effect except on himself. But standing in the wings . . . the bystander sees things neither actor nor audiences notices.

Above all, he sees differently from the way actors or audiences see. Bystanders reflect—and reflection is a prism rather than a mirror; it refracts."

This theme, that he was more onlooker than participant, came up often in Drucker interviews. At first I thought it was little more than false modesty. But that was the same story he told to his last day. He told *BusinessWeek*'s John Byrne six months before he died that he did his best work in the 1950s and characterized his work since then as "marginal."

The John Byrne interview, conducted so close to his death, was revealing. On that day Drucker was in poor spirits and poor health. Perhaps that's why he was so negative about himself and his legacy. He had been plagued by abdominal cancer and had broken his hip in 2004 (I was still corresponding with Drucker when that injury occurred and he had written one short letter to me from his hospital bed). "One doesn't pray for a long life but for an easy death" was something he said repeatedly.

What Drucker maintained until the end was that what interested him more than anything was people—*other* people. He wrote that he had never met a single, uninteresting person. No matter how conformist, how conventional, or how dull, people become fascinating the moment they talk of the things they do, know, or are interested in. Everyone then becomes an individual."

"I'm totally uninteresting," he told that same *BusinessWeek* reporter. "I'm not very introspective," he answered when asked about his legacy. "What I would say is I helped a few good people be effective in doing the right things. I'm a writer, and writers don't have interesting lives. My books, my work, yes. That's different," he said despondently.

Someone who took such an interest in other people had to be shaped by them, I reasoned. If I was ever going to understand the man behind the words I would need to understand the people who shaped *him*, the people who were the greatest influences in *his* life.

Fortunately, Drucker liked to talk of other people—in our interview, in his books, and in his numerous articles. He made it clear which leaders he admired the most, the least, and the ones that were clearly corrupt or worse.

On the world stage, he gave the highest grades to the Winston Churchill of World War II, and not the Churchill who preceded the war. That Churchill was on the sidelines, and wasn't yet a factor. Drucker believed that events can make men, or at least events can bring out the best in men.

On the topic of presidents, he admired Harry Truman for how he grew into the job, but had far less respect for Franklin Delano Roosevelt and John F. Kennedy. He maintained that FDR was insecure and threatened by strength, so would seek to undercut anyone around him whom he viewed as a potential threat.

He claimed John Kennedy had more charisma than any other president but got almost nothing done. These are controversial and unpopular views, as both of these presidents, particularly Roosevelt, were among the century's most celebrated leaders.

But Drucker's observations about presidents or prime ministers tell us little about who he was; for that, we need to go back and explore the lives of the people who touched Drucker the most, the ones he remembered and wrote about many decades later.

The following five summaries represent important turning points in Drucker's life. They are not meant to compose even a brief biography. Instead, they are meant as brief snapshots, taken at different times, each teaching him something important—and us as well, as bystanders to *his* life.

The Beginning

Drucker's early years have become an oft-told tale. He grew up in a quiet Viennese suburb. His parents were well educated: Adolph, his father, was a "high government official" and his mother, Caroline, was a doctor. Young Peter grew up in a "semidetached" house designed by a noted Austrian architect, Josef Hoffmann.

The most noteworthy aspect of Drucker's early years was the soirees that were hosted by his parents. Two to three times each week, philosophers, intellectuals, lawyers, government officials and others would make their way to Drucker's drawing room. Among the most noteworthy of these impressive guests were members of the Vienna Circle.

This elite group of philosophers included some of the best and brightest in Austria, and they held similar beliefs and view of the world. They believed that "experience is the only source of knowledge; and second, logical analysis performed with the help of symbolic logic is the preferred method for solving philosophical problems."

One regular guest was the noted economist Joseph Schumpeter, one of the most important economists of the twentieth century and someone who had a business relationship with Drucker's father. It was Schumpeter who first wrote of the importance of entrepreneurs in society, crediting them for inspiring technological change and innovation. Later, at Harvard, he argued that large corporations sparked innovation, since it was these firms that had the resources needed for research and development.

Peter Drucker met Sigmund Freud when he was only eight. Freud and Drucker's family ate lunch at the same restaurant and they vacationed near the same lake.

"Remember today," his father told young Peter, "you've just met the most important man in Austria, and perhaps in Europe."

"More important than the Emperor?" Peter asked.

"Yes, more important than the Emperor," confirmed his father.

Peter never forgot that day, nor did he forget what he learned from the parties that were held in his home. While the level of discourse was quite lofty for someone so young, Peter was permitted to participate in these get-togethers (that is, until his bedtime at 9:30 p.m. By 10:30, everyone had to leave to catch the last train to the city center). Drucker would later say "that was my education" when referring to the spirited discussions that took place those evenings.

It was certainly the *beginning* of his education. There, in the beliefs and theories of leading thinkers such as those in the Vienna Circle and Joseph Schumpeter, one can see the roots of Drucker's own philosophies begin to take shape. Also, Drucker's keen interest in so many subjects—art, philosophy, religion, science, law, sociology, business, literature—is a reflection of the diversity of people who regularly made their way to the Drucker home to share their thoughts and passions on those subjects.

There were many others who touched Drucker throughout his life. To document them all would require a book of its own, and indeed, Drucker wrote that book, *Adventures of a Bystander*, to which much of this Epilogue owes its origins. Like many of his books, it isn't the easiest read, despite the many jewels that are there when one looks hard enough.

Drucker calls *Bystander* a "book of short stories, each standing by itself. But it is also an attempt at a social portrait—an attempt to capture and convey the essence, the flavor, the feel, of what very few people now alive can possibly imagine: interwar Europe, the New Deal years, and America right after World War II."

Despite that ambitious goal, which the book achieves, I found something else in that book. I found *Drucker*—the one who eluded me in his other books, his articles, in our interview, and in the other books written about him. For it is among these people, in "other people's lives," that one can discern how such a singular figure like Drucker emerged.

"A Stupid Old Woman"

The first chapter of Drucker's *Adventures of a Bystander* is devoted to his grandmother, a character even the most imaginative screenwriter could not conjure up.

Peter's grandmother became a widow at age forty. She suffered from a great many ailments, including rheumatic fever, which damaged her heart; a bad case of crippling arthritis, which left her joints swollen, especially her fingers; and if those were not bad enough, she was nearly deaf. None of these health issues, however, kept her from getting around. Peter remembered his grandmother rushing all over the city with a big black umbrella she used as a cane and a shopping bag that "weighed as much as she did."

Everyone called her Grandmother, even her daughters and nieces. All the family members had their favorite grandmother stories, all of which revealed an eccentric old woman who always did things her own way, no matter how ridiculous they seemed.

That is why she was known as "the family moron," a moniker

she never denied. In fact, she called herself "a stupid old woman" every chance she got, and confirmed it with the questions she asked and the things she did.

For example, although her husband had left her "a fortune," the Austrian inflation had made her "as poor as a church mouse." But even Drucker's father, whom Drucker called "the family economist," could not explain the concept of inflation to her, no matter how hard he tried.

One more example: because of her ever-worsening economic situation, she was reduced to living in two small rooms. When her things no longer fit, she packed many of her belongings into huge shopping bags and took them to her bank. By then, she had only "a few pennies" left in her account. But her late husband had founded the bank and had been its chairman until his death, so she was treated with the respect that was owed to the late chairman's widow.

When she tried to deposit the contents of her shopping bags into her account, the bank manager explained that people could not deposit "things" into a bank account, only money. Grandmother called the man "mean and ungrateful," closed her account, stormed out with her pennies in hand, and opened a new account in another branch—of the same bank!

But "stupid old woman" did not tell the full story of this woman Drucker obviously cherished. She treated everyone with respect, and always remembered the things that mattered most to the people she met, even if a long time had passed since she had last seen them.

Even the prostitute outside of her apartment was treated with Grandmother's usual brand of courtesy. Everyone ignored the woman, but Grandmother always bid Miss Lizzie a good evening, asked her if she was warm enough on cold nights, and even climbed up and down five flights of stairs to bring her medicine.

No one thought Grandmother clever, but she was able to do things that others couldn't. For example, before 1918 no one in Austria needed papers to get anywhere. But after the breakup of the "old Austria," the government made it as difficult as possible and required everyone to have both a passport and a visa to get anywhere. Getting such documents meant standing on lines for hours on end, only to have to do it all over again after being told that you needed more or different papers.

But Grandmother short-circuited the system. Drucker's father was the senior civil servant at the Austrian Ministry of Economics, so she went to the ministry's messenger and somehow found a way to get not one, but four different passports (British, Austrian, Czech, and Hungarian).

When Drucker's father learned of what she had done, he threw a fit: "The ministry's messenger is a public servant and must not be used on private business," he yelled. Grandmother responded calmly: "I know that. But am I not a member of the public?"

But her best story took place the last time Drucker saw her alive. Drucker tells it with pride in *Bystander*. It was the early 1930s and she and Peter were riding a streetcar when a young man with a swastika got on board. Grandmother could not sit still, so she got up and poked the young Nazi with her umbrella, and said: "I don't care what your politics are; I might even share some of them. But you look like an intelligent, educated young man. Don't you know this thing"—and she pointed to the swastika—"might give offense to some people? It isn't good manners to offend anyone's religion, just as it isn't good manners to make fun of acne. You wouldn't want to be called a pimply lout, would you?"

Drucker wrote that he had held his breath in fear of what would happen. Even then Nazis were "trained to kick an old woman's teeth without compunction." But to Drucker's relief, the young Nazi removed the swastika and put it in his pocket. When he got off the streetcar a few minutes later, he tipped his hat to the old woman. While the entire family was aghast at the chances she took, they were both impressed and amused by her actions.

At the time, Drucker's father was trying, to no avail, to have Nazis banned from Austria. "If only we can have Grandmother ride all streetcars, all the time," he laughed.

It was then that Drucker began to question Grandmother's status as "a stupid old woman."

"It wasn't only that her stupidity worked," he wrote. "She did get through the postwar boundaries without having to stand in line for days on end; she made the grocer reduce his prices; and she got the lout to take off his swastika." Drucker explained that he had been "arguing with Nazis for years and never seen the slightest results. Here was Grandmother appealing to manners, and it worked."

Drucker pondered that while she was not clever, he slowly began to wonder if she had "wisdom rather than sophistication or cleverness or intelligence. Of course she was funny, but what if she was also right?"

Drucker concluded that Grandmother "practiced basic values. And she tried to inject them into the twentieth century, or at least into her sphere of it."

Drucker's Greatest Teachers

Peter Drucker, who would turn out to be a first-class educator, and who, as a professor, turned down Harvard and other world-class institutions, never had a better teacher than the two he had when he was in the fourth grade.

They were Miss Elsa and Miss Sophy, and they were sisters.

Miss Elsa had been the principal since the school he attended opened twelve years earlier. She was Drucker's homeroom teacher as well, and that meant that she worked with him for four hours every day, six days a week.

Miss Elsa explained that the school term would start with three weeks of quizzes and tests to gauge how much each of the students knew. Drucker was frightened at the prospect, but it turned out to be fun. That was because she had each student grade themselves or one another.

At the conclusion of the three-week test period Miss Elsa

sat down with each of her students for a one-on-one talk and asked each what they thought they did well.

She agreed with Drucker that he was a very good reader, but she told him that he needed more practice in composition. So she made a deal with him. He was to write two compositions each week, one topic that she would assign, and one that he would come up with on his own.

Last, she told Drucker that he underestimated his performance in math. She told him that he was actually good at arithmetic, which surprised the young student. He had been told by other teachers that he was bad at math. "Your results are poor. But not because you don't know arithmetic," she explained patiently. "They are poor because you are sloppy and don't check. You don't make more mistakes than the others; you just don't catch them. So you'll learn this year how to check—and to make sure you do, I'll ask you to check all the arithmetic work of the five children sitting in your row and the row ahead of you."

Miss Elsa told Drucker that they would meet once a week to check his progress. If a student did something totally out of line, like cheat repeatedly, Miss Elsa would give that guilty child a "tongue-lashing that flayed us alive." But that kind of dressing down was never done in front of others, it was always done in private.

Miss Elsa would focus on the strengths of each of her students, and then set both short-term and long-term goals to develop those strengths. Then, and only then, would she focus on weaknesses. She then provided the kind of feedback that would allow students to improve their own performance and "direct themselves" (which would later become a key Drucker tenet— he contended that employees should be given the feedback to direct themselves, for "all development is self development").

At the start of the year she told Peter that she would never lavish praise on him for the things he excelled at, and would compliment him only rarely. But she would "bear down on us like an avenging angel if we did not improve or advance in areas that needed strengthening, and especially areas in which we had potential."

In describing what made Miss Elsa great, he explained that "she was not in the least 'child-focused'... she was interested in their *learning*. Yet she knew every child's name and every child's characteristics and above all, his or her strengths, within the first week.... We did not love her, but we worshipped her."

"Miss Sophy, by contrast, was totally child-focused," wrote Drucker. The children "swarmed all over her." Drucker explained that there was always a student in her lap, and even the biggest kids were not afraid to run to her when something was wrong.

Children brought Miss Sophy their problems and their triumphs, and despite the fact that she could never remember a child's name, she was always there for a pat or a hug, praise or congratulations.

She taught arts and crafts out of a studio that Drucker described as a magical place that included easels, crayons, brushes, hand tools, hammers, child-sized sewing machines—everything a child could hope to find in such a place. Miss Sophy,

wrote Drucker, would let the children try out most anything—
"always willing to help but never offering advice or criticism."

Miss Sophy taught her students "non-verbally and silently."
When a child was drawing or woodworking, she would watch
for a few moments before taking her very small hand (she was a
tiny woman) and guide the child's hand until he or she got it.
Or if a child could not draw, she would take the crayon or brush
and paint "a purely geometric, non-objective figure that yet
bore all the elements that make a cat a cat." Suddenly the student would see the cat amid the shapes and start laughing. That
would bring a smile to Miss Sophy's face, which was the "only
praise she ever gave, but one that was pure bliss to the beholder."
She never, ever criticized a child, no matter what.

Drucker called Miss Elsa "the very perfection of the Socratic
method," and Miss Sophy "a Zen master."

Drucker then made a stunning admission. He said that he
might have gone into teaching in any event, because he needed
an income, but without these two incredible teachers, it would
have been unlikely.

"Without Miss Elsa and Miss Sophy in my memory I would
have resisted teaching myself." They taught Drucker that "teaching and learning, of high quality and with a high level of inten-
sity and enjoyment, are possible. These two women set
standards and they gave examples."

The Monster and the Lamb

By the spring of 1932, Drucker had made up his mind to leave Frankfurt, for he knew what it would mean to Germany if the Nazis came to power the next year.

Drucker went to Germany in 1927 to work in an export company in Hamburg. A little more than a year later he moved to Frankfurt, first to work in a merchant bank for a European branch of a Wall Street company. But the crash of 1929 quickly extinguished that career, and instead he found himself as a financial journalist on Frankfurt's most popular newspaper. Drucker rose rapidly and in two years was promoted to a senior position in charge of foreign and economic news.

Drucker said that his success was not due to him, but to the state of post–World War I Europe: "In my early twenties I found myself a senior editor of a big newspaper, not because I was so good but because the generation ahead of me simply did not exist. There were no thirty year olds when I was twenty; they were lying in the cemeteries of Flanders and Verdun, Russia and the Isonzo . . . few people today—least of all in America—can realize how World War I decimated Europe's leadership."

Drucker was good, and even managed to get a doctorate in international and public law by 1931 (at age twenty-two).

As he worked full time as a reporter, he also taught law and wrote other pieces for magazines. Feeling that he had outgrown the newspaper, he even began to search for a new job. But at the same time he prepared to leave Germany. The prospect of Hitler and the Nazis was unthinkable for Drucker, who came up with a plan that would "make it impossible for the Nazis to have anything to do with me," he explained, "and equally impossible for me to have anything to do with them."

Drucker decided to write a book, no, something smaller, "a pamphlet really, about Germany's only political philosopher, Friedrich Julius Stahl," who was also a Jew. A positive book on this defender of freedom represented, in Drucker's words, "a frontal attack on Nazism."

As Drucker had anticipated, the book never saw the light of day. It was burned by the Nazis. Still, it was important for Drucker to pursue it: "It made it crystal-clear where I stood; and I knew I had to make sure for my own sake that I would be counted, even if no one else cared," Drucker explained.

Drucker published another small book, little more than a pamphlet: *Die Judenfrage in Deutschland*, or *The Jewish Question in Germany*, four years after the Stahl book, and it was also burned. The only copy that still exists is in the Austrian National Archives, with a swastika marked on it.

Drucker was not surprised that Hitler won the election and came to power on January 31, 1933. He had feared Hitler and the Nazis for years, and had correctly predicted in 1927 (just after Hitler *lost* that election) that the Nazis would one day come to power.

One noteworthy event convinced Drucker once and for all that he had to leave Germany. He was on the faculty of Frankfurt University and although he never went to a single faculty meeting, he attended the first one hosted by the newly installed Nazi commissar. The meeting was a total disaster.

The first announcement was that all Jewish faculty would be immediately banned from the university and fired without salary. Then it turned far worse when the Nazi commissar launched into a tirade of profanity. He threatened every faculty member: follow orders or go to a concentration camp. Drucker made up his mind to leave Germany within two days.

When he got home he was grateful that the page proofs for his Stahl book were there. He read the proofs that night. By ten he was exhausted, and was surprised when someone knocked on his door. He said his "heart missed a beat" when he saw a Hitler storm trooper on his doorstep. He was slightly relieved when he recognized the person to be a man named Hensch, a colleague at the newspaper where he had worked (the *Frankfurter General-Anzeiger*).

The two memorable things about Hensch, thought Drucker, were his beautiful Jewish girlfriend (whom he had broken up with when Hitler came to power) and his membership in both the Communist and Nazi parties.

Hensch had heard that Drucker had also quit the newspaper (in addition to his teaching position), and tried to talk him out of leaving the newspaper. Drucker would have none of it.

Then Hensch switched gears, and burst into an emotional tirade. He told Drucker how much he envied him, that he was not "clever" like Drucker, and only wished he could leave. But he said he could not. He wanted money and status and power, and said that because he had a low membership number in the Nazi Party (which meant more power), he would now be somebody. "Mark my word," he told Drucker, *"you'll hear of me now."*

That's when Drucker saw the future. He had known that Hitler would make good on the promises he had made in his book *Mein Kampf* (a book that was a failure when it was published in 1925 but became a best seller that sold almost as well as the Bible after Hitler took over). The book was a prescription for the carnage and genocide that would grip Europe in the years ahead. "And suddenly I had a vision of things to come, of the horrible, bloody, and mean bestiality that was descending on the world."

Drucker predicted the Holocaust in his first book (not a management book), *The End of Economic Man: A Study of the New Totalitarianism*, published in 1939. But he knew the night Hensch visited him that Hitler would succeed in creating a killing machine. Hensch was typical and unimpressive, and his ordinariness meant that there were hundreds of thousands, even millions more, just like him, who would willingly succumb to Hitler's form of institutional killing.

Drucker arrived in the United States in 1937, and he never heard from Hensch again. But just after the Nazis were defeated in 1945, a short piece in *The New York Times* captured his attention:

Reinhold Hensch, one of America's most wanted Nazi war criminals, committed suicide when captured by American troops in the cellar of a bombed-out house in Frankfurt. Hensch, who was deputy head of the Nazi SS with the rank of Lieutenant General, commanded the infamous annihilation troops and was in charge of the extermination campaign against Jews and other enemies of the Nazi state ... he was so cruel, ferocious, and bloodthirsty that he was known as "The Monster" (Das Ungeheuer) even to his own men.

Drucker escaped Germany in 1933, went to Vienna, as planned, and a few weeks later went to England. He knew one person there: a highly respected German journalist named Count Albert Montgelas. Before leaving Vienna, Drucker sent him a note and was pleasantly surprised when a telegram arrived from the count asking Drucker to come as quickly as possible: "I need you."

When Drucker arrived, the count was packing up his office, having also resigned just after the Nazis gained power.

Montgelas was gravely concerned that a celebrated reporter from New York, Paul Schaeffer, was going to accept a position offered to him: editor of the *Berliner Tageblatt*. For more than fifty years the *Tageblatt* had enjoyed the same reputation as *The New York Times* or *The Times* in London, Drucker explained. Schaeffer had reported on FDR from the time he was governor of New York through his presidential inauguration.

Schaeffer was no one's idiot. He knew better than anyone what the Nazis were up to, but he thought that he could make a difference: "It's precisely because this is such a horror that I have to accept this job," he explained. "I am the only man that can prevent the worst. The Nazis will need me and the *Berliner Tageblatt* ... they'll need someone like me who knows the West, who knows whom to talk to and who's listened to. They'll need me because not one of them knows anything about the outside world."

Montgelas asked Schaeffer if he was afraid of being used by the Nazis, to "give them a front of respectability and to bamboozle the outside world." Schaeffer even had a written offer from Henry Luce (on *Time* stationery) to be chief European correspondent for *Time*, *Fortune*, and a future picture magazine (which would be *Life*), with a hint that he would be in line for the top job. Schaeffer's wife begged him to take the Luce job.

But Schaeffer would hear none of it. He felt he "owed" his mentor, the previous editor of the *Tageblatt*, a Jew who had been fired by the Nazis as soon as they took over. And he owed his country as well. So he took the job.

From the start, the Nazis used him precisely as Drucker and Montgelas feared. "Title, money and honors were heaped on him," Drucker explained. "The Nazi press pointed to his appointment as editor-in-chief [to show] that all the stories about the Nazis and their treatment of the press that had appeared in foreign newspapers were just dirty Jewish lies. Whenever news of Nazi atrocities filtered out, Schaeffer was dispatched to the

foreign embassies in Berlin or to a meeting with foreign corre-
spondents to assure them that these were 'isolated excesses'
that would not be allowed to recur."

Two years after Schaeffer took the job, after both he and the
Berliner Tageblatt had been completely exploited by the Nazis,
"both were liquidated and disappeared without a trace," reported Drucker.

In a chapter Drucker called "The Monster and the Lamb,"
Drucker reflected on the meaning of these two individuals:
Reinhold Hensch and Paul Schaeffer. He quoted the German-
American philosopher Hannah Arendt, who, in her book on
Nazi war criminal Adolf Eichmann, wrote of "the banality of
evil." Drucker called that "a most unfortunate phrase."

"Evil is never banal. Evil-doers often are," asserted Drucker.
"Evil works through the Hensches and the Schaeffers precisely
because evil is monstrous and men are trivial . . . and because
evil is never banal and men so often are, men must not treat
with evil on any terms—for the terms are always the terms of
evil and never those of man. Man becomes the instrument of
evil when, like the Hensches, he thinks to harness evil to his
ambition; and he becomes the instrument of evil when, like the
Schaeffers, he joins with evil to prevent worse."

Drucker ends the piece by asking which did more harm, the
monster or the lamb? "Which is worse, Hensch's sin for the lust
of power or Schaeffer's hubris and sin of pride? But maybe the
greatest sin is neither of these two ancient ones; the greatest sin
may be the new twentieth-century sin of indifference, the sin of

the distinguished biochemist who neither kills nor lies but refuses to bear witness when, in the words of the old gospel hymn, 'They Crucify My Lord.' "

These are just a few of the people—and events—who helped to make Peter Drucker what he became. There are countless others. I selected these few, because these individuals had such a pervasive influence on him. They touched him in ways others didn't.

These individuals affected far more than Drucker's brain, they affected his humanity. That theme is ever present in Drucker's writings and his life. They also provided him with an expansive, rather than limiting, view of the world.

The people who attended Drucker's parents' parties when he was a child taught him to take an interest in a great many things, including politics, art, science, law, economics, and more. They opened his mind, preparing him for all of the things that he would do later.

His grandmother was, of course, far more than a "stupid old woman"; she was infused with humility and wisdom. She also exhibited great courage, a quality that Drucker had in spades. Both his grandmother and, later, Drucker would challenge Nazism in their own ways. His grandmother on a streetcar and he with his banned manuscripts.

Miss Elsa and Miss Sophy taught Drucker that teaching could be a magical profession. By his own admission, he doubted that he would have devoted his life to it had he not had these two teachers way back in the fourth grade.

Each taught him to focus on strength. Miss Elsa taught him to focus on the end result, learning, as results were what mattered most. To learn one needed to know what one did best and those areas in which more work was needed. Miss Elsa's testing, followed by the student's self-grading, helped each student to discover the strengths he or she needed for self-development. That became a key Drucker management tenet. In *The Practice of Management* he wrote: "Each manager should have the information he needs to measure his own performance and should receive it soon enough to make any changes necessary for the desired results."

Drucker lived through two world wars, something that few contemporary writers experienced. His incidents with the monster and the lamb made Fascism and Nazism personal. He had a front-row seat at the Nazis' rise in power in the late 1920s through Hitler's victory in 1933. He saw the future that night when Hensch, later known as The Monster, came to visit him the night before he left Germany. He considered Nazism a social phenomenon, something that caused academia to reject his book *The End of Economic Man*, much later.

He also saw how the great sin of hubris can destroy as forcefully as a monster like Reinhold Hensch. Paul Schaeffer's belief—only I could prevent the worst—led to a disastrous outcome. Despite the best intentions, he quickly became an accomplice who played right into the hands of the Nazis. He was their front man on the world stage, one who gave the Nazis just enough legitimacy for them to continue their war and mass genocide. By masking what was actually going on under Nazi rule in Europe, he might have helped other world leaders justify their neutrality.

In the end, Drucker considered the lamb as destructive as the monster. Both formed vivid images in his mind. In knowing these two men, he knew exactly what he was against. In all of his writing, teaching, and consulting, he sought to spread knowledge and learning, build people up, enhance our institutions, and show other people how they can do the same. He was a humble man all his life, never giving in to the sin of hubris or pride. When he made a mistake he admitted it, learned from it, and moved on.

According to Drucker biographer Elizabeth Haas Edersheim, Drucker's view from the front-row seat at the events in Europe in the first decades of the twentieth century determined his future: "Peter's passion was the direct outgrowth of having witnessed Europe's economic free fall in the 1930s," she wrote in *The Definitive Drucker*.

"The failures and collapse that he wrote about in the 1930s," she continued, "were, to his mind, directly connected to poor business and government management. He was convinced that the lack of a viable economic engine in Europe is what brought Hitler to power."

"The rise of Fascism and Communism," she explained, "only confirmed Drucker's view of the critical need for vibrant businesses in any society. 'Without economic opportunity,' he wrote in 1933, 'the European masses realized for the first time that existence in this society is governed not by what is rational and sensible, but by blind, irrational, and demonic forces.' He then went on to say that the lack of an economic engine isolates individuals and they become destructive."

Drucker's first two books (not counting the two pamphlets banned by the Nazis) touched on these themes. *The End of Economic Man*, Drucker's first book, was published in the spring of 1939. When published, it received an incredible amount of attention, especially for a first-time writer. It accurately predicted the coming Holocaust.

Churchill lavishly praised the book, and after he became prime minister, he made sure a copy was included in the kit issued to every graduate of every British officers' candidate school. (The other book included in the kit was Lewis Carrol's *Alice's Adventures in Wonderland*. Drucker said somebody there had a sense of humor.)

Although the book wasn't published until just before World War II started in 1939, Drucker had begun to write it far earlier, just a few weeks after Hitler came to power in 1933. The way this book was rejected by the academic community foreshadowed Drucker's entire career. In the 1960s and 1970s the book was ignored by the scholarly community, explained Drucker. That was because it did not fit either of the two prevailing views of

Nazism: that it was either a "German phenomenon," or "the last gasp of dying capitalism."

Instead, the book "treated Nazism—and totalitarianism altogether—as a *European* disease, with Nazi Germany the most extreme, most pathological manifestation and with Stalinism not being much better or much different." That was "not politically correct," commented Drucker wryly.

The second reason Drucker felt that the book was ignored was because it "treats a major social phenomenon as a *social* phenomenon. This is still largely considered heresy," he wrote in 1994.

The second book that Drucker would write, the one that directly preceded his years studying GM and the publication of his first business book (*Concept of the Corporation*, 1946), was *The Future of Industrial Man* (1942). In the book Drucker argues "that the basic institution of industrial society has to be both a community that gives status, and a society that gives function, and that it needs its own special institution to do so. I did not yet call this institution an 'organization.'"

Drucker explained that no one used the word *organization* until after World War II, and that he might have been first to use the term in *Concept of the Corporation*. In *Industrial Man*, he argues that the emerging industrial society is different from what preceded it, "different structurally from nineteenth-century and early twentieth-century society and has different challenges, different values, different opportunities."

In these first two books we can recognize the Drucker who would invent the field of modern management as we know it today. He saw Nazism and totalitarianism as a "social" phenomenon. In *The Future of Industrial Man*, he saw the coming industrial society, the coming organizations (even though no one called them that yet), as something quite distinct from the institutions of the late 1800s and early 1900s. And the contrast would go beyond structure or form—they would have different opportunities and values.

In the first hour of my interview with Drucker, he spoke of how he established management as a *social* institution. Nobody had seen the corporation as a social institution. "It didn't have the most lasting impact, but the greatest impact," asserted Drucker.

Drucker told me that had it not been for the two earlier books, *Concept of the Corporation* would never have been published. The same publishing house published *Concept*, but only because the first two had done so well. Had *Concept* not been published, the Peter Drucker we now know—the inventor of management—may have chosen another career path. That's an outcome I don't even want to think about.

Acknowledgments

This book could not have been written without the cooperation of Peter F. Drucker. When Dr. Drucker learned of the book I intended to write, he offered to help me in any way he could, and made good on his offer several times over. I am forever in his debt, and will remember him as the great man he was.

There are several other people who read the manuscript early on; some made suggestions on improving it, and all were kind enough to provide written testimonials. Included in this esteemed group are: Warren Bennis, Philip Kotler, Robert J. Herbold, Barbara Bund, Jack Zenger, Christopher Bartlett, and Bill McDermott. I thank them here for taking the time out of impossible schedules to read and comment on the manuscript.

The Portfolio team at Penguin is simply second to none. It all started with Adrian Zackheim, who is not only the founder of Portfolio, but also my editor (and boss!). As far as publishers go, it was he alone who recognized the value of a book that humanized Drucker while summarizing his many key concepts in a single volume.

Courtney Young did what she always does, a superb job editing and making just the right suggestions. I also thank Will Weisser and Maureen Cole, Daniel Lagin for the perfect interior design, Noirin Lucas for spearheading the production effort, and Joseph Perez for his inspired cover design.

I also owe a debt of gratitude to my agent Margret McBride and her terrific team—Donna Debutis, Faye Atchison, and Anne Bomke. The book is a much better one for their efforts.

I have the most supportive family in the world. My wife, Nancy, and twin boys, Noah and Joshua, always gave me the time to write, even if it meant having one boy on my left arm, and the other on the right. They are my life, and give meaning to everything I do. I am truly blessed to have them.

And lastly, to my mother and father, Trudy and Barton, who made me what I am today.

Sources

This book could not have been completed without the cooperation of Peter F. Drucker. In addition to the extensive interview he granted me, he was also generous enough to give me permission to quote from any and all of his books (and any book written about him). From *Concept of the Corporation* to *Management Challenges for the 21st Century*, his words and wisdom are the very fabric of this book and I am forever in his debt. Many of the quotes in the book came directly from the interview I had with him on December 22, 2003, at his home in Claremont, California. A few other quotes were taken from letters we exchanged before and after the interview. However, the bulk of the Drucker quotes in the book were excerpted from his books, listed below.

The books that were the most helpful were *The Practice of Management*, his 1954 crowning achievement that was years ahead of its time, and perhaps the best management book ever written. Others include *Managing for Results* (Harper & Row, 1964) and *The Effective*

Executive (Harper & Row, 1967), two of his best and earliest works. *Management Challenges for the 21st Century*, (HarperCollins, 1999) one of Drucker's last works, was invaluable in providing insight into his latest thinking on a variety of critical topics. *Adventures of a Bystander* (HarperCollins, 1991), Drucker's sole attempt at a memoir, was the predominant source of the material that appears in the epilogue.

There were other articles and books that were also invaluable in the compilation of this book. Below you will find an exhaustive list of the sources used in researching and writing it. In addition, I would like to acknowledge here several of the most helpful sources: John Byrne's excellent *BusinessWeek* cover story on Drucker, "The Man Who Invented Management," written days after his death, was very helpful in filling in some key, poignant details about Drucker and his thoughts in the final months of his life.

Elizabeth Haas Edersheim's *The Definitive Drucker* (McGraw-Hill, 2007) also helped to fill in some of the gaps regarding Drucker's earliest writings (among other topics).

Rich Karlgaard's interview with Peter Drucker, "Peter Drucker on Leadership," which appeared on Forbes.com, November 19, 2004, was also quite helpful in providing Drucker's thoughts on a variety of topics a year after our interview took place (and a year before his death).

John Micklethwait and Adrian Wooldridge's *The Witch Doctors: Making Sense of the Management Gurus* (Times Books, 1996, 1997), was a superb reference book, which provided several excellent quotes and background material.

Other books that were particularly helpful were Andy Grove's *Only the Paranoid Survive* (Doubleday Currency, 1996), Clayton Christensen's *The Innovator's Dilemma* (Harvard Business School Press, 1997), Larry Bossidy and Ram Charan's *Execution* (Crown Business, 2002), John Zenger and Joseph Folkman's *The Extraordinary Leader* (McGraw-Hill, 2002), and Marcus Buckingham and Donald Clifton's *Now, Discover Your Strengths* (Free Press, 2001).

List of Sources

Please note: for a complete quote-by-quote, source-by-source listing, go to my Web sites: JeffreyKrames.com or insidedruckersbrain .com.

Beatty, Jack. *The World According to Drucker*. New York: Free Press, 1998.

Bezos, Jeff. 1997, 1998, 1999, 2000 annual letter to Amazon.com shareholders.

Bossidy, Larry, and Ram Charan. *Execution: The Discipline of Getting Things Done*. New York: Crown Business, 2002.

Buckingham, Marcus, and Donald Clifton. *Now, Discover Your Strengths*. New York: Free Press, 2001.

Byrne, John. "The Man Who Invented Management." *BusinessWeek*, November 28, 2005.

Christensen, Clayton. *The Innovator's Dilemma: When New Technologies Cause Great Firms to Fail*. Cambridge: Harvard Business School Press, 1997.

Collins, Jim. *Good to Great: Why Some Companies Make the Leap … and Others Don't*. New York: Collins, 2001.

———. From the foreword in *The Daily Drucker: 366 Days of Insight and Motivation for Getting the Right Things Done*. New York: Collins, 2003.

Colvin, Geoffrey. "Blue Cross Blue Shield." *Fortune*, October 16, 2006.

Drucker, Peter F. *The End of Economic Man*. New York: Heinemann, 1939. Transaction edition, 1994.

———. *The Future of Industrial Man*. New York: The John Day Company, 1942.

———. *Concept of the Corporation*. New York: The John Day Company, 1946.

———. *The Practice of Management*. New York: Harper & Row, 1954 (copyright renewed in 1982).

———. *Managing for Results*. New York: Harper & Row, 1964.

———. *The Effective Executive*. New York: Harper & Row, 1967.

———. *Technology, Management and Society*. New York: HarperCollins, 1970.

———. *Management: Tasks, Responsibilities, Practices*. New York: Harper & Row, 1974.

———. *The Changing World of the Executive*. New York: Times Books, 1982.

———. *Innovation and Entrepreneurship*. New York: HarperCollins, 1985.

———. "The Coming of the New Organization." *Harvard Business Review*, January–February, 1988.

———. *Managing the Non-Profit Organization*. New York: Harper-Collins, 1990.

———. *Managing for the Future*. New York: Plume, 1993.

———. *The Post-Capitalist Society*. New York: HarperCollins, 1993.

———. *Adventures of a Bystander*. New York: HarperCollins, 1998.

———. *Peter Drucker on the Profession of Management*. Cambridge: Harvard University Press, 1998.

———. *Management Challenges for the 21st Century*. New York: Collins, 1999.

———. *The Essential Drucker: The Best of Sixty Years of Peter Drucker's Essential Writings on Management*. New York: Collins, 2001.

———. *Managing in the Next Society*. New York: St. Martin's Press, 2002.

———. Letter to Jeffrey A. Krames, November 14, 2003.

———. "Clayton Christensen on Peter Drucker." Thought Leader's Forum, Peter F. Drucker Biography, The Peter F. Drucker Foundation for Nonprofit Organizations.

Drucker, Peter F., and Joseph A. Maciariello. *The Effective Executive in Action: A Journal for Getting the Right Things Done*. New York: Collins, 2005.

Edersheim, Elizabeth Haas. *The Definitive Drucker*. New York: McGraw-Hill, 2007.

Grove, Andrew S. *Only the Paranoid Survive*. New York: Doubleday Currency, 1996.

———. "Andy Grove on Intel." *Upside*, October 12, 1997.

———. Academy of Management speech, San Diego, California, August 9, 1998.

————. Interview with John Heilemann. *Wired* magazine, June, 2001.

Humby, Clive, Terry Hunt, and Tim Phillips. *Scoring Points: How Tesco Continues to Win Customer Loyalty*. London: Kogan Page, 2007.

Karlgaard, Rich. Peter Drucker interview with Rich Karlgaard, "Peter Drucker on Leadership." Forbes.com, November 19, 2004.

Kennedy, Carol. *Guide to the Management Gurus*. London: Random House, UK, fifth edition, 1991.

Krames, Jeffrey A. *What the Best CEOs Know*. New York: McGraw-Hill, 2003.

Lafley, A. G., from the Foreword, in Edersheim, *The Definitive Drucker*.

Magee, David. *How Toyota Became #1*. New York: Portfolio, 2007.

Micklethwait, John, and Wooldridge, Adrian. *The Witch Doctors: Making Sense of the Management Gurus*. New York: Times Books, 1997.

Montgomery, David. *Fall of the House of Labor*. Boston: Cambridge University Press, 1989.

O'Toole, James. *Leadership A to Z: A Guide for the Appropriately Ambitious*. New York: Jossey-Bass, 1999.

Rothschild, William E. *The Secret to GE's Success*. New York: McGraw-Hill, 2007.

Spector, Robert. *Amazon.com: Get Big Fast*. New York: HarperBusiness, 2000.

Tichy, Noel M., and Stratford Sherman. *Control Your Destiny or Someone Else Will*. New York: Doubleday Currency, 1993.

Watson, Thomas J. *Father, Son & Company: My Life at IBM and Beyond.* New York: Bantam Books, 1991.

Welch, Jack. *Jack: Straight from the Gut.* New York: Warner Books, 2001.

Zenger, John H. HR.com Webcast, July 1, 2005.

Zenger, John H., and Joseph Folkman. *The Extraordinary Leader: Turning Good Managers into Great Leaders.* New York: McGraw-Hill, 2002.

Index